Nurturing the Shy Child

| | | | | | | | | | | | | | | | | | | | | | | | | | | | | | | | | | | | | | | | | | | | | | | | | | | | | | | | | | | | | | | | | | | |

Barbara G. Markway, Ph.D.

and

Gregory P. Markway, Ph.D.

Nurturing the Shy Child

Practical Help for Raising Confident and

Socially Skilled Kids and Teens

THOMAS DUNNE BOOKS ✹ NEW YORK

ST. MARTIN'S GRIFFIN

THOMAS DUNNE BOOKS.
An imprint of St. Martin's Press.

www.thomasdunnebooks.com

www.stmartins.com

Library of Congress Cataloging-in-Publication Data

Markway, Barbara G.
    Nurturing the shy child : practical help for raising confident and socially skilled kids and teens / Barbara G. Markway, Gregory P. Markway.
       p. cm.
    ISBN-13: 978-0-312-32978-5
    ISBN-10: 0-312-32978-4
    1. Bashfulness in children. 2. Child rearing. I. Markway, Gregory P. II. Title.

BF723.B3M37 2004
649'.1—dc22

2004056112

First St. Martin's Griffin Edition: August 2006

10 9 8 7 6 5 4 3 2 1

To Kayla and Sherry

Note to the Reader

||||||||||||||||||||||

This book is intended to serve as an informational resource only and should not be taken as psychological or medical advice.

Contents

||||||||||||||||||||||||

Acknowledgments

We had always heard that working with a large New York publisher would be an impersonal experience, yet we have had the opposite experience. Our warmest thanks go to all of the wonderful people at Thomas Dunne Books/St. Martin's Press who have consistently made us feel as though we are collaborating with a group of friends.

Our special thanks to Thomas Dunne, for believing in our books; to Carin Siegfried, our editor, for her attentiveness and kindness. We wish her well in her future endeavors, and we appreciate the work of our new editor, Peter Joseph. Thanks also go to Steve Snider, jacket designer, for creating an image that captures the feel of our book. Our copy editor, Cynthia Merman, was invaluable in shaping the book into a polished, finished product. We also want to acknowledge our son, Jesse, for his wit and wisdom; our parents, Bill and Erika Gerth and Ruby Markway, for their unwavering support and interest in our careers; and Susan Williams and Sister Caroline Markway, for sharing their years of classroom experience.

Introduction
Hope and Help Are Near
by Barbara G. Markway, Ph.D.

||||||||||||||||||||||

I'VE STUDIED shyness and social anxiety all my life. Part of my hard-earned knowledge comes from real-life experience. Do you remember that kid who sat in the back of the class who never spoke? That child was me. I grew up painfully shy and suffered through my twenties with much social anxiety. I know what it's like to have plenty to say but be afraid to speak up. I know what it's like to feel my face flush and my heart race out of control when I'm in a social situation. I know what it's like to make decisions based on what I think I can manage, rather than what I truly want to do. And I know what it's like to feel horrible about myself for these things.

Fortunately, I've made great strides in overcoming my social anxiety. I'm still quiet compared to some—that's just who I am. But I no longer limit my life because of fear. I say what I want to say and do what I want to do. I go out into the world and use my talents and don't worry so much about what others think of me. Best of all, I'm free of the low self-esteem and depression that often go hand in hand with social anxiety.

The other part of my knowledge comes from education. I have a doctorate in psychology and nearly twenty years of clinical experience. I've worked with people of all ages who suffer from severe shyness and social anxiety, and I know the pain these problems can cause. More important, I know the tremendous advances we've made in understanding and helping people with these problems.

When my husband, Greg, and I wrote *Painfully Shy: How to Overcome Social Anxiety and Reclaim Your Life,* we were talking to and about shy and socially anxious adults, although we included a chapter on helping shy children. Since the book's publication, we've been overwhelmed with positive feedback from readers who've been gracious enough to let us know we met a need. A common theme we've heard from readers has gone something like this: "I wish my parents had this information when I was growing up. Maybe I would've been spared some of the hardship I've endured." Indeed, I've thought the same thing myself. How nice it would have been if severe shyness had been recognized as a serious issue some forty years ago. But that wasn't the case. As you'll read later, social anxiety disorder is relatively new on the scene as a diagnostic entity. This doesn't mean it didn't exist before—we just didn't have a name for it.

Thus, our goal in writing *Nurturing the Shy Child* is to provide parents, teachers, guidance counselors, therapists, and other concerned adults with the information and tools they need to help shy, socially anxious kids as early as possible. Research studies indicate that social anxiety disorder tends to develop early, often during adolescence. In fact, many of our clients tell us they can't remember a time when they weren't painfully shy. If we can prevent some of the suffering that accompanies social anxiety disorder, we'll have accomplished something important.

My husband and coauthor, Greg, also a psychologist, has helped many people overcome long-standing fears and anxieties and go on to live full and productive lives. He plays an important role in our writing projects. While I'm the one who usually sits at the computer and writes the initial drafts, Greg's keen perspective offers plenty of suggestions for additions and revisions. Although we created this book as a team, we know it can be confusing to switch back and forth between us, alerting the reader to who is saying what. Thus, this book is primarily written in my voice. "We" refers to both Greg and me, "I" refers to me (Barb).

While we're on the subject of writing style, we also realize it can be cumbersome to write in a gender-neutral way. Sometimes we use the pronoun "he" and sometimes we use "she." As both boys and girls experience shyness and social anxiety, we use a variety of examples that reflect this. All of the names have been changed to protect confidentiality. To further protect privacy, some examples are composites of a number of different children with whom we've worked.

One last note: This book sometimes uses the terms "shyness" and "social anxiety" interchangeably. We cover definitions and distinctions in the next chapter, but some of the distinctions really are just a matter of semantics. This book will show you how to help your child whether she is simply shy in some situations or whether she experiences anxiety in nearly all social situations. The principles for facing fear and managing anxiety are the same. Obviously, your wish as a parent or teacher is to nurture your child to reach his full potential—as the army says, to help him be all that he can be. Our wish, and our belief, is that this book will be a powerful aid in that process.

Nurturing the Shy Child

|||||||||||||||||||||||||||||||||||||||||||||||||||||||||||||||||||||||||||||||

CHAPTER 1

How Shy Is Too Shy?

Understanding Painful Shyness and
Social Anxiety in Kids

WHEN I first met eight-year-old Austin, I had to greet him under the table in the waiting room. There he sat with his freckles and red, curly hair, arms locked around his knees, eyes glued to the ground. As his parents tried to coax him out from under the table, I could tell this was a scared little guy. "Hey, Austin. I've got some toys in my office. You can play while I talk with your parents," I said. His blue eyes glanced up as I told him he wouldn't have to say a word if he didn't want to. His parents sighed with relief as Austin scooted out from under the table and followed us back to my office.

In talking with his parents, I asked about Austin's interests. I learned that he loved baseball. He and his dad watched major league games on television together, and they played catch in the backyard almost every evening. This year Austin was finally old enough for "coach pitch" baseball. When the day came for the first practice, Austin fell apart. He clutched his stomach saying it hurt, and he begged his parents not to make him go. "I knew he wasn't sick because he acted fine moments before I said it was time to leave," his mother told me.

The whole season went poorly and everyone became frustrated in the process. Austin cried before every practice and threw a major temper tantrum before each game. Some of the episodes were so severe that his parents carried him off the floor kicking and screaming to put him in the car. He didn't talk with the other boys on the team, and he could barely look the coach in the eye. Although Austin apparently had some talent from all the practicing he had done in the backyard with his father, he froze on the field and couldn't perform.

The problems they had with Austin and baseball that summer were eerily familiar, his parents told me. The previous fall Austin said he wanted to be in Cub Scouts. They signed him up, but when the first meeting rolled around, Austin cried and had a fit, refusing to go. His parents didn't push scouting and let him quit after a few traumatic attempts to get him to attend.

His parents explained that Austin could be quite a chatterbox at home and got along well with his brother and sister. When he was at school, however, it was a different story. During the parent-teacher conferences throughout the year, his teacher repeatedly expressed concern that Austin was "so quiet" and never participated in any group discussions. She also told them he played by himself at recess. He didn't seem to know how to join in with the other children. In addition, Austin frequently complained of stomachaches at school and asked to be sent to the nurse's office.

While many of their friends and relatives told them Austin was "just shy," his parents weren't convinced. I was glad they brought Austin to see me. From many years of working with children like Austin, I knew he wasn't "just shy." He was *painfully shy*. His shyness was interfering with his life. It kept him from fun things like baseball and Boy Scouts, and it prevented him from being happy at school. Eventually, if left untreated, his severe shyness could lead to other issues, such as academic problems, low self-esteem, and depression.

The technical term for the condition Austin suffers from is *social anxiety disorder,* or *social phobia* as it's sometimes called. In the rest of this chapter, you'll learn what social anxiety is, at what point it becomes a disorder, and the common symptoms children with this problem are likely to experience. You'll also have the opportunity to complete a questionnaire to determine if your child may have social anxiety disorder and where his or her particular problems lie. Perhaps the most important information you'll take from this chapter is the realization that you're not alone. As was the case for Austin's parents, it can be a relief to know your child's problem has a name and that help is near.

WHAT IS SOCIAL ANXIETY?

SOCIAL ANXIETY IS a universal experience, one that's necessary for survival. It was easier to see its survival value in previous times, when people had to band together to hunt food, build shelter, and ward off enemies. Social anxiety served the function of keeping people close to the "pack." To veer off from the group was to risk death.

Even now, we've evolved in such a way that we're motivated to remain a part of the group. We want to be accepted. We want to fit in. Thus, some social anxiety is normal and beneficial. After all, people who *never* care about others' opinions are often not very pleasant to be around and have a completely different set of problems.

But what exactly is social anxiety? It's the experience of apprehension or worry that arises from the possibility, either real or imagined, that one will be evaluated or judged in some manner by others. Sometimes it's easier to explain what social anxiety is by listing some ordinary, everyday examples:

- embarrassment after spilling a drink
- "stage fright" before a big performance
- awkwardness while talking to someone you don't know well
- nervousness during a job interview
- feeling jittery before giving a speech

These are common experiences almost everyone has had at one time or another. Children, too, naturally experience some social anxiety throughout their day-to-day lives. Because most children attend school, many situations that elicit social anxiety are for them particular to their environment:

- being called on by the teacher
- giving a report in class
- reading aloud
- eating in the school cafeteria
- writing on the blackboard
- using school restrooms

Since social anxiety is so universal, how do you know where your child's reactions fall? Are they within the range of normal? Or, like Austin, does social anxiety pose more of a problem? In other words, how can you tell when social anxiety becomes social anxiety disorder—a clinical diagnosis?

RECOGNIZING SOCIAL ANXIETY DISORDER

MENTAL HEALTH PROFESSIONALS use *The Diagnostic and Statistical Manual of Mental Disorders—Fourth Edition (DSM-IV)* to make diagnostic decisions. While it's not a perfect system, diagnoses are important for a number of reasons. Without a name for the problem, research vital to understanding and developing effective treatments for it simply doesn't take place. On a practical level, if you try to receive mental health services for a problem that has no diagnosis, you're not likely to get your insurance to pay.

Let's look at the specific criteria that must be met for a clinical diagnosis of social anxiety disorder. Then we'll discuss some of the nuances involved in diagnosing social anxiety disorder in children. The *DSM-IV* says an individual with social anxiety disorder

- shows significant and persistent fear of social situations in which embarrassment or rejection may occur
- experiences immediate anxiety-driven, physical reactions to feared social situations
- realizes that his or her fears are greatly exaggerated but feels powerless to do anything about them
- often avoids the dreaded social situation—at any cost

Someone may fear just one or a few social situations—public speaking is a common example—in which case the problem is referred to as a *specific* or *discrete* social phobia. In contrast, *generalized* social anxiety disorder exists when a person is afraid and avoids many, or most, social situations.

Once these basic criteria are met for a diagnosis of social anxiety disorder, the individual symptoms can vary, but they generally fall into three categories: the cognitive or mental symptoms (what you think); the physical reactions (how your body feels); and the behavioral avoidance (what you do). Let's look at these three areas in more detail.

The mental anguish. People with social anxiety disorder are plagued with negative thoughts and doubts about themselves:

- Do I look okay?
- Will I know what to talk about?
- Will I sound stupid or boring?
- What if other people don't like me?

The fear of possible rejection or disapproval is foremost in socially anxious people's minds, and they scan for any signs that confirm their negative expectations.

The cognitive symptoms of social anxiety disorder are often not as evident in children, especially young children. They may react with intense anxiety yet not be able to verbalize what is upsetting them. This was the case for six-year-old Claire. Whenever it was time to go someplace, for example, Sunday school or a friend of the family's house, Claire balked. She usually began by stating, "I don't want to go." When her parents questioned her further about why she didn't want to go, she'd reply, "I don't know. It will be boring." That's what her parents heard a lot—"It will be boring." With further questioning, Claire's tone and volume became more distressed. She'd beg and plead not to go but could never give what her parents considered a good reason to justify her discomfort.

The physical distress. Many people don't realize that actual physical discomfort can accompany social anxiety. For example, someone may experience a panic attack in a social situation, in which they feel an acute and severe rush of fear and anxiety, accompanied by some or all of the following symptoms: shortness of breath, tightness or pain in the chest, racing heart, tingling or sensations of numbness, nausea, diarrhea, dizziness, shaking, and sweating. Panic attacks usually come on quite quickly, build to a peak in approximately five to twenty minutes, and then subside. It's not uncommon for people to say that their panic attacks last a lot longer; however, it's probably the aftereffects of the attack that they're feeling, such as residual anxiety and increased alertness to bodily sensations, rather than the panic attack itself.

Adolescents are much more likely to experience panic attacks than are younger children. In fact, panic attacks in young children are unusual. Rather, younger children with social anxiety typically complain of headaches and stomachaches, although they may have other physical symptoms as well.

Regardless of which particular physical symptoms your child experiences, anxiety is never pleasant. Having one's body in a state of constant alert takes its toll and can lead to low energy, muscle tension, irritability, and sleep disturbances.

Also keep in mind that the physical symptoms are usually real.

Many parents think their children are merely making up excuses, and while this can sometimes be the case, more typically these kids have truly worked themselves up into a state of physical discomfort.

The toll of avoidance and other behavioral reactions. It's human nature to try to avoid pain and suffering. From an evolutionary perspective, we're "hardwired" either to fight or flee a dangerous situation. It's no surprise, then, that people with social anxiety disorder tend to avoid or painfully tolerate situations that they believe will cause them harm. This might mean never attending a party. It might mean having few, if any, friends. It might even mean dropping out of school.

The consequences of avoidance naturally vary depending on the person and the severity of his or her anxiety. In all cases, though, people with social anxiety disorder limit their choices out of fear. Decisions in life are based on what they're comfortable with rather than what they truly want to do.

Because children are not as able to avoid the situations they fear (for example, they *have* to go to school), parents are likely to witness more behavioral symptoms in these anxious children, such as:

- crying
- tantrums
- freezing
- clinging
- staying close to a family member

Unfortunately, these kids are often labeled as "oppositional" and "defiant." This is usually not the case. When you consider the fact that children don't enjoy the same freedom as adults to avoid the situations they fear, their behavior makes more sense. When an anxious child perceives that he's being backed into a corner and forced into something frightening, "acting out" with tears or tantrums seems like the only option.

Thirteen-year-old James is exceedingly bright, but he's never been athletically inclined. To make matters worse, he has exercise-induced asthma. He's always had problems in physical education classes. He frequently gets teased by other kids, and to make matters worse, last year his PE teacher humiliated him in front of the other kids because he couldn't run a mile. At the beginning of the next school year, James dressed out and did as he was told in PE, to the best of his ability. He'd always been a well-behaved student who tried to get along well with others. But one day, another kid called him "fat," and James lost it. He knocked the kid to the ground and started punching him, and both boys ended up in detention. From that day on, James had had enough. He refused to dress out in PE and told his school counselor he didn't care if he got an F. Someone who didn't look closely at the situation might have concluded that James was a troublemaker. But this was hardly the case.

Let's look briefly at two extreme examples of the behavioral avoidance associated with social anxiety—*selective mutism* and *school refusal*. Children with selective mutism do not speak at school or in other public places where others might hear them, or they speak only in a barely audible whisper. These children speak freely and easily, however, at home with family members. This condition used to be called "elective mutism," reflecting the thinking that these children were deliberately not speaking, perhaps being stubborn or trying to get attention. Current theories argue that the problem is *not* elective. Rather, it's as if these children's voice boxes are frozen with fear, preventing them from communicating with words.

School refusal applies to children who have a pattern of avoiding or refusing to attend school. Although children can refuse to attend school for a variety of reasons, in many cases social anxiety is the root cause. We discuss selective mutism and school refusal in Chapters 9 and 10.

FREQUENTLY ASKED QUESTIONS REGARDING THE DIAGNOSIS OF SOCIAL ANXIETY DISORDER IN CHILDREN AND ADOLESCENTS

EVEN FOR A seasoned professional, the diagnosis of social anxiety disorder in children and adolescents can be complex due to developmental factors and the frequency of more than one anxiety disorder involved. In addition, here are a few other issues to keep in mind.

My son has always been socially awkward. His language was delayed and he still hasn't caught up to other children his age. Could he have social anxiety disorder?

Most likely, no. Social anxiety disorder is an appropriate diagnosis only for children who have developed age-appropriate language skills and who demonstrate the ability to interact socially. A child with social anxiety disorder frequently is outgoing and charming around close family members yet has difficulty interacting around unfamiliar children and adults. Children with developmental disorders such as autism or Asperger's disorder would not be diagnosed with social anxiety disorder.

Won't my child grow out of this?

To diagnose social anxiety disorder in children, the problems must have persisted for at least six months. This helps rule out the possibility that your child is simply going through a phase. Once your child's difficulties have gone on for at least six months and are serious enough to warrant a diagnosis of social anxiety disorder, it's best not to take a wait-and-see approach. By this point unhealthy patterns of avoidance and withdrawal probably have become habitual and aren't likely to be changed without some concerted effort.

My child acts fine around kids her own age, but she is extremely shy around adults. She hides behind my leg and refuses to talk. Is this common?

Because adults represent authority and are in a position of power, it's not uncommon for children to be uncomfortable and quieter around them. For this reason, to be diagnosed with social anxiety disorder children must demonstrate anxiety with both peers and adults.

My seven-year-old son seems to have no awareness that his fears are unreasonable. Does that matter?

The *DSM-IV* guidelines for diagnosing social anxiety disorder state that the person must realize that his or her fears are greatly exaggerated. This criterion does not need to be met for children, however. Given their less mature cognitive development, we would not expect them to have insight into the unreasonableness of their fears and reactions.

My child has a bad case of test anxiety. Could this be a part of social anxiety disorder?

Yes. Test anxiety can be a part of the social anxiety spectrum. Drs. Sam Turner and Deborah Beidel, two prominent researchers in the area of social anxiety, found that 24 percent of test anxious children also met the criteria for social anxiety disorder. If a child has only test anxiety, it is considered a *specific* form of social anxiety. If the test anxiety goes along with other social fears, it is part of *generalized* social anxiety disorder. In addition, test anxiety may be unrelated to social anxiety. For example, if a child has a severe learning disability in math, you would obviously expect some anxiety before a math test. Many of the treatment strategies we discuss throughout this book can help children overcome test anxiety.

SHYNESS AND SOCIAL ANXIETY IN CHILDREN AND ADOLESCENTS: A VERY COMMON PROBLEM

SHYNESS IN CHILDREN and adolescents is by no means uncommon. According to Jerome Kagan, Ph.D., a professor of psychology at Harvard University, roughly 10 to 15 percent of kids in kindergarten through eighth grade are very shy, 25 percent tend to be outgoing and sociable, with the rest falling somewhere in between. In a separate study, Bernard Carducci, Ph.D., a shyness expert at Indiana University, has found that the percentage of shy teens is about the same as shy adults—around 40 percent.

According to Jerilyn Ross, president of the Anxiety Disorders Association of America, about 13 percent of youth aged nine to seventeen suffer from anxiety disorders, making them the most common mental disorder in young people. Depending on the research study reviewed, between 5 and 6 percent of children and adolescents have generalized social anxiety disorder.

In addition, the prevalence of problems that coexist in children with a primary diagnosis of social anxiety is similar to those in adults. A research study conducted by Drs. Beidel and Turner found that in children with social anxiety disorder

- 20 percent had other specific phobias
- 16 percent had generalized anxiety disorder
- 8 percent had depression
- 16 percent had attention deficit hyperactivity disorder
- 16 percent had learning disabilities

These figures illustrate the fact that children with social anxiety disorder often exhibit numerous problems and complex symptoms. In fact, another respected researcher, Dr. Murray Stein, admits that it can be difficult to diagnose social anxiety disorder in children and thus it's difficult to obtain a true picture of how many youth are affected. This is because of the numerous interwoven fears some children have. He uses the term "anxious triad" to describe how separation anxiety disorder, generalized anxiety disorder, and social anxiety disorder often overlap in children. We discuss these disorders and their overlap with social anxiety throughout the book and more specifically in Chapter 11.

THE SPECTRUM OF SHYNESS AND
SOCIAL ANXIETY DISORDER

AS WE MENTIONED, making a diagnosis of social anxiety disorder in children and adolescents is not always simple. Part of what makes it a challenge is that shyness and social anxiety disorder actually exist on a continuum. Let's look at a number of brief examples.

Shy but basically secure and successful. Sixth grader Vanessa fits into the category of someone who is shy but also someone who is basically secure and successful. She has always been on the quiet side. In fact, every teacher throughout her elementary school years commented that she was "reserved." She doesn't like giving oral book reports or having to stand in front of the class, but she is able to do so when required. She has a few good friends, although not a very wide circle. She attends parties of kids she knows well, although she frequently turns down invitations for slumber parties.

Her parents accept her shy temperament and have never made a big deal of it. They are both on the quiet side themselves and seem to understand that this is simply who Vanessa is. They try to encourage her to break out of her comfort zone and try new things, put they're not overly pushy. She is usually reluctant at first, but with support, she participates in a few extracurricular activities, such as Girl Scouts.

Vanessa's parents worried that the transition from grade school to middle school would prove challenging for her. Indeed, Vanessa was a bit "stressed out" for the first month of school. She complained that the hallways were too crowded and she didn't like switching classrooms for every subject. But in a month or so, she got into the swing of things and now seems to be faring quite well.

Shy but showing some problems. Like Vanessa, Sydney is cautious in new situations. She likes to check everything out before jumping into anything. She is always the one on the playground watching the other kids from the perimeter. She might eventually join in if she knows the kids and the game they are playing. At home, Sydney is content to play by herself for hours. Creative and with a keen imagination, she likes to sit and draw or play make-believe games with her dolls.

Unlike Vanessa's situation, however, Sydney's parents are outgoing and love to entertain. They frequently have other families over for casual dinner parties, and this makes Sydney very uncomfortable. Her mother becomes upset with Sydney for not coming out of her room to talk with their guests. At times, she thinks Sydney does this to make her mad. She has even punished Sydney for not being "polite" to their guests.

I first saw Sydney when she was in the third grade. Her parents were sure there was some deep-seated reason why their daughter wasn't more sociable. Similarly, Sydney didn't feel very good about herself. She realized she wasn't measuring up to her parents' expectations. She wished she could be more outgoing, but she simply didn't feel comfortable with her parents' friends. She didn't know what to say or how to act.

Sydney's parents were truly concerned about what they perceived as their daughter's lack of social interest. They didn't understand that this was part of her temperament—not something she was doing on purpose. I helped her parents learn to accept Sydney's quiet personality style and not to put so much pressure on her to be different. This went a long way toward helping Sydney feel better about herself. I also worked with Sydney to develop some social skills and some much-needed confidence.

Specific social anxiety disorder. Rob is in the eighth grade and just a little bit shy. He's always had a lot of friends and done well in school. He loves music and has been in the orchestra for years. He's developed into quite a talented violinist, and his orchestra teacher selected him to perform a solo in the spring concert.

This has made Rob a nervous wreck. The concert isn't for several months, and already Rob is having trouble sleeping, has lost his appetite, and is considering dropping out of the orchestra.

Rob's reaction may sound extreme, but we've worked with people of all ages where this sort of situation occurs. The anxiety leading up to a feared event (what we call *anticipatory anxiety*) is so uncomfortable that it doesn't seem worth it to the person to go through all that misery. Rather than endure the discomfort, he withdraws from the feared event. We've also worked with people who have had a panic attack during a performance situation and vowed never to go through that experience again, thus quitting some activity they were good at and enjoyed.

Mild to moderate generalized social anxiety disorder. Megan is now in high school and has been shy all her life. Her parents have been supportive and tried to encourage her, yet quite a few odds were stacked against Megan. Her family has a strong history of anxiety and depression on both sides. Megan's father is in the military and they have had to move every few years, which has made it difficult for her to make friends.

Megan gets lower grades than she'd like in school. Although she is of at least average intelligence, because she always sits in the back of the class and never asks any questions, she sometimes misses important points the teacher is making. She's also lost out on extra credit toward her grade based on class participation.

In addition, Megan suffers from physical symptoms of anxiety. For example, when she's in class, if it appears they'll have to go around the room and take turns answering questions, she feels as if she's going to have a panic attack. Her heart beats wildly, she feels flushed, and she has difficulty concentrating. She's sure she won't be able to speak coherently when her turn comes. Sometimes she even feels dizzy and worries she might faint. Of course, fainting in class would prove embarrassing to Megan, and worrying about that possibility just makes matters worse.

Severe generalized social anxiety disorder. The distinctions among the categories are somewhat arbitrary in nature. If Megan's symptoms progressed, she could easily fit in the severe generalized social anxiety disorder category. Here we include children who have selective mutism or school refusal. We also include children and teens who've become depressed as a result of their social anxiety. For example, kids like Megan can become isolated, lonely, and even hopeless. Children who have numerous physical symptoms or panic attacks and kids who avoid most social situations also fit into this category.

As we said, the categories themselves aren't important. What is important is understanding the range of problems that can exist so that you're better able to understand your child's particular situation. In addition, rest assured that the strategies presented in this book can help you help your child, regardless of where he or she falls along the continuum of shyness and social anxiety.

For the child who is shy but basically secure and successful, this book will strengthen what you already know and what you're already doing correctly with your child. In addition, feel free to skip ahead to Chapter 8 for ideas on making friends and feeling comfortable in large groups. For the child who falls somewhere along the middle of the continuum, you can learn to be a knowledgeable coach who can help your child reach his or her full potential. And if your child falls on the end of social anxiety disorder, there is a lot you can do to help. But keep in mind that you may also need a psychologist who is trained in treating childhood anxiety disorders to guide you through the process.

Look at the diagram below. Where do you think your child's problems fall?

Shy but secure	Shy with problems	Specific social anxiety disorder	Mild-moderate generalized social anxiety disorder	Severe generalized social anxiety disorder

The good news in all this is that you're not alone. Many parents of children who are shy and socially anxious have learned skills to help their children grow into socially confident and capable adults. The next step is gaining more specific information into the nature and extent of your child's social concerns.

DOES MY CHILD HAVE
SOCIAL ANXIETY DISORDER?

BELOW IS AN informal screening questionnaire that covers many of the situations commonly feared by children with social anxiety disorder, as well as typical symptom patterns. By going through these questions, you will gain a snapshot of your child and his or her problems. You can answer the questions yourself based on your knowledge of your child. Or, depending upon the age of your child and how motivated and cooperative he or she is, you can ask for your child's help. Consider also asking your child's teacher for input. Teachers have a lot of firsthand knowledge about how your child behaves in school—information that you quite possibly wouldn't be able to obtain on your own.

These are the situations my child is likely to complain about or is known to avoid.

- ❏ Answering questions in class
- ❏ Raising hand in class
- ❏ Writing on the blackboard
- ❏ Musical or drama performances
- ❏ PE class (a lot of social and performance pressures)
- ❏ Giving an oral report
- ❏ Eating in the cafeteria
- ❏ Asking the teacher a question
- ❏ Using the school restrooms (not due to fear of germs)
- ❏ Doing anything that involves getting out of one's seat in class and drawing attention to self (e.g., getting up to sharpen pencil)
- ❏ Participating on team sports

- ❏ Going to parties
- ❏ Informal conversations with other kids
- ❏ Hanging out by the lockers
- ❏ Riding the school bus
- ❏ Going to a friend's house
- ❏ Inviting a friend over
- ❏ Using the telephone
- ❏ Participating in a sleepover
- ❏ Going to the store
- ❏ Ordering food at a restaurant
- ❏ Talking to neighbors or other adults
- ❏ Joining in with kids at recess
- ❏ Doing things while being watched
- ❏ Taking tests
- ❏ Dating or going to dances
- ❏ Other: _____
- ❏ Other: _____
- ❏ Other: _____

These are the things I hear my child tell himself or herself before, during, or after a social situation. *(Young children often don't know what they're thinking, so you may not be able to answer this section very easily.)*

- ❏ I don't fit in.
- ❏ No one likes me.
- ❏ I don't have any friends.
- ❏ I'm stupid.
- ❏ I'm ugly.
- ❏ I can't do it.
- ❏ I'm boring.
- ❏ It's going to be horrible.
- ❏ I won't know what to say.
- ❏ People will notice I'm nervous.
- ❏ Other: _____
- ❏ Other: _____

These are the physical symptoms my child is likely to experience when anxious. *(Many of these symptoms can be internal and not visible to someone else. Your child may look okay but actually be quite anxious. In addition, children experience shame about their physical symptoms and go to great lengths to hide them. Some symptoms, like blushing, are impossible to hide. These type of symptoms—those that can't be disguised— often cause kids the greatest concern.)*

❑ Headaches
❑ Stomachaches
❑ Diarrhea
❑ Nausea
❑ Feeling like he or she might vomit
❑ Blushing
❑ Sweating
❑ Shaking
❑ Hot flashes/cold flashes
❑ Muscle tension
❑ Heart palpitations or racing heart
❑ Tightness in chest
❑ Shortness of breath
❑ Feelings of weakness (e.g., legs feel like Jell-O)
❑ Light-headedness/dizziness
❑ Choking sensations, lump in throat, dry mouth
❑ Feelings of unreality (like in a fog)
❑ Other: _____
❑ Other: _____

My child experiences panic attacks, either in social situations or in anticipation of them. *(A panic attack is a sudden surge of intense fear and anxiety, usually accompanied by several or many of the above physical symptoms. It usually reaches a peak in five to twenty minutes before subsiding.)*

❑ Yes
❑ No

My child is likely to experience panic attacks in these situations:

_____

My child experiences panic attacks approximately _____ times per week.

These are the behavioral reactions I notice in my child when he or she is confronted with a feared social situation.

❏ Throwing a temper tantrum
❏ Having a crying fit
❏ Refusing to go or participate
❏ Clinging, staying close to a family member's side
❏ "Freezing"—literally acting as if frozen by fear, not moving, not speaking
❏ Avoiding eye contact with others, looking down
❏ Asking for excessive and repeated reassurance
❏ Acting agitated or irritable, begging to go home early

Other key questions to ask yourself about your child's reactions to feared social situations.

❏ Do your child's problems interfere with academic (school) functioning?
❏ Does your child's anxiety interfere with making and keeping friends?
❏ Is your child missing out on fun activities that many children of the same age enjoy?
❏ Do people comment on your child's excessive shyness?
❏ Do you spend time worrying about your child's shyness?
❏ Is shyness or social anxiety affecting how you feel about your child, or how your child feels about himself or herself?
❏ Is your family environment affected by your child's anxiety? Do you tiptoe around, trying not to set him or her off?

Now review your answers. As you do, refer back to pages 12–15 where we discuss the criteria for and categories of social anxiety disorder. Also keep in mind some of the differences that exist in diagnosing children and adults (e.g., children don't have to realize their fears are unrealistic and excessive). Although this is not a substitute for an evaluation with a mental health professional, you will likely be able to tell whether your child's anxiety problems fall into this diagnostic category. If you think your child has more problems than are covered in this questionnaire, refer to Chapter 11, which covers other problems commonly associated with social anxiety disorder.

WHAT DO I DO NOW?

IF YOU FEEL overwhelmed at this point, that's natural. We've covered a lot of ground, and it can be disconcerting to think that your child has a "disorder." In the chapters ahead, we cover each of the areas in the questionnaire and show you proven techniques to help your child overcome the mental, physical, and behavioral symptoms of social anxiety disorder.

Many of you will make good progress by reading this book and following the strategies presented. There are times, however, when parents need to consult a professional about their child's problem. Appendix A, "Seeking Professional Help," will guide you on how to recognize such times.

It can be painful for some parents to admit they need help with their child or that their child has problems. But there's nothing to be ashamed of. Start by taking the blame off yourself and giving up the guilt—you have not failed your child. Channel your energy into seeking the help your child needs. Realize that now, more than ever, there are ways to minimize the harmful effects of unchecked social anxiety. Together, we'll teach your child the skills he needs to master his social anxiety and to lead the rich life he was meant to live.

CHAPTER 2

Is This My Fault?

*A Model of What Causes
and Maintains Social Anxiety*

I F THE burning question on your mind right now is, "What caused this?" you're not alone. This is the number one question parents ask after learning their child has social anxiety disorder. It's a natural reaction. Knowing the reason for a problem provides a sense of control and predictability. Equally important, understanding what causes something points the way toward change.

Unfortunately, many parents tend to blame themselves. There is no reason for this. Although parenting styles may sometimes play a role in the development of social anxiety disorder, this is almost always only one piece of the puzzle. Many experts don't even discuss causes, preferring instead to talk about "predisposing factors." In other words, they look at what aspects of a person's life—be it faulty genes or negative experiences—make it more or less likely that social anxiety will develop.

Still, knowing what causes social anxiety is just the beginning. Once social anxiety takes hold in a child, different factors perpetuate the problem. Things like worrying too much and avoiding situations explain why, without intervention, painfully shy kids tend to stay painfully shy. Sadly, it's often the very things kids do to cope with anxiety—sitting in the back of the class so the teacher won't call on them, for example—that maintain the fear over the long run. Later in the chapter, we show how these and other misguided attempts at calming one's nerves make matters worse. But first, let's look at why social anxiety strikes in the first place.

WHAT CAUSES SOCIAL ANXIETY?

TWO MAJOR FACTORS—biology and environment—increase the chances a child will develop social anxiety disorder. Because we're organizing a large amount of material, we discuss these factors one by one. Keep in mind, however, that your child's biological makeup and life experiences combine and interact in such a way that it's difficult, if not impossible, to separate the two forces.

Brain strain: The role of biology in social anxiety. Hope Longwell stands out in my mind because her success hinged on an understanding of her biological makeup. Hope was eight years old when her parents called for an initial appointment. Her case was somewhat unusual in that she had already been correctly diagnosed with social anxiety disorder and had tried cognitive-behavioral treatment, the psychological treatment of choice.

During our first meeting, Mr. and Mrs. Longwell elaborated on Hope's situation. "We did everything the previous therapist asked us to do. We helped her practice relaxation techniques. We monitored difficult situations and had her rate her fear levels. We encouraged her to do things she was afraid of—in small steps," her mother explained. Despite what appeared to be good effort on everyone's part, Hope made only minimal progress and still experienced extreme anxiety in social situations. Mr. Longwell asked me, "We tried the therapy diligently for nearly a year. Why didn't it work?"

I needed more information before I could answer that question. I had a hunch, though, that Hope's biological makeup was a major stumbling block.

Over the next hour, I learned a lot about Hope and her extended family. Mrs. Longwell told me that her mother was a nervous person. She worried about everything and suffered from "dizzy spells," as she called them. She often bolted for the door while gasping, claiming she needed more air. The more Mrs. Longwell described her mother, the more it sounded as if she might have panic disorder, another common anxiety condition. She also told me that her uncle, her mother's brother, was extremely shy and had never married. I wondered to myself if this uncle might be socially phobic.

I asked other questions: What had Hope been like as a baby? At what age did she walk and talk? What were her first school experiences like?

Mrs. Longwell described Hope as a "fussy" baby. She had cried a lot and didn't soothe easily. She also resisted any regular eating or sleeping schedule. Many things bothered her: loud noises, unfamiliar people, and new situations.

Hope didn't attend preschool, and she was rarely left with a babysitter. As a result, the beginning of kindergarten was the first time she'd been away from her parents. Mrs. Longwell told several stories about the terrible time she'd had trying to get Hope to school. Hope ripped several of her mother's blouses by clutching her so tightly when she tried to leave the classroom. Their morning routine went like this for months.

The Longwells also described Hope's previous therapy. From what they could tell me, and from reviewing Hope's records, it sounded like she received excellent treatment. Furthermore, I could find no fault with this family's efforts. Just as they'd told me, the records showed that they regularly attended their appointments and completed all of the outside assignments.

Yet Hope was still a "bundle of nerves." True, they acknowledged that she had made some progress—she could carry out a few basic social tasks if she was really forced into it. But time after time her body reacted as if she were about to fall off a cliff. The intense physical reaction didn't change much, even with the best, most appropriate psychological treatment.

At this point, I offered my general impressions of the situation. I suspected that Hope's inborn, biological makeup led her to see danger quickly and easily, often when there really was nothing to fear.

"For Hope, anxiety is almost as natural as breathing," I explained. "It's like a needle stuck on a scratch in a record—your brain gets stuck in a fearful, anxious groove and can't get out. Even with all of your good efforts in therapy, Hope's brain didn't unlock and allow her body to grow comfortable with social situations. Instead, she remained on edge, prepared for attack."

I also told the Longwells that anxiety runs in families—perhaps she'd inherited her fearful tendencies. Her wary nature as an infant and her separation problems as a young child further confirmed a biological component to her anxiety. I stressed that it wasn't Hope's fault. It wasn't her parents' fault. It wasn't anyone's fault. I suggested a referral to a physician for a medication consultation and reassured Hope and her parents there was an excellent chance medicine would help.

Mr. and Mrs. Longwell were hesitant at first. They understandably weren't sure they wanted their child on medication. They needed some facts. They needed to know the scientific basis for what I was telling them.

To explain the benefits of medication, I shared with them some of the latest findings about the role biology plays in the origins of social anxiety. The next several pages provide an overview of this research. Most scientific studies have looked at three major areas: genetics, neurobiology, and temperament. As you read about these physical factors, think about how Hope's story illustrates them. Also consider your own situation and how your child's social anxiety might have developed. Later, you'll have an opportunity to answer some questions to further clarify your thoughts about these issues.

GENETICS. One of the strongest ways to test for the genetic basis of a disorder is through the study of twins. Monozygotic, or identical, twins share the exact same genetic makeup. In contrast, dizygotic, or fraternal, twins are no more genetically similar than are any other siblings. In these studies, if a certain condition occurs more commonly in identical twins as compared to fraternal twins, this higher rate of occurrence indicates a genetic component. Unfortunately, twin studies are difficult to arrange and few have looked specifically at social anxiety disorder.

A large twin study conducted in 1992, however, examined the genetic basis for all anxiety disorders. The psychiatrist Kenneth Kendler, a specialist in genetics at the Medical College of Virginia, along with his colleagues found that social phobia did, in fact, occur more commonly in identical twins. Among identical twins, in cases where one twin had social phobia, the other twin also suffered from the disorder 24.4 percent of the time. In contrast, among fraternal twins, if one twin had social phobia, 15 percent of the twins also had it. These results indicate that genetics is a factor in at least some cases of social anxiety disorder. Most likely, though, there is not a gene specific to social anxiety. Rather, what's inherited is probably a vulnerability to develop anxiety; other factors must be present before social anxiety emerges.

In addition to twin studies, family studies are a way to test for the genetic basis of a disorder. This type of research examines how disorders cluster among family members. Sometimes, clients are simply asked whether they know of other family members with psychological problems. Other times, researchers interview family members directly to determine the presence of a particular disorder. Some research includes only adult relatives; other studies also include children.

An interesting study conducted in 1996 by Professor Cathy Mancini and her associates at McMaster University in Canada examined the presence of anxiety disorders in the children of socially anxious parents. They found that 49 percent of the children had at least one anxiety disorder, 30 percent had overanxious disorder, 23 percent had social phobia, and 19 percent had separation anxiety disorder. Although there were some problems with this research, results from most of these studies support the idea that anxiety runs in families. Genetics likely plays some role in this.

NEUROBIOLOGY. Have you wondered if your child has a chemical imbalance? Although the term "chemical imbalance" is a bit unscientific and imprecise, many people relate to it. It's understandable: When anxiety strikes, one's body feels completely unbalanced, and it seems that there must be something physically wrong.

Actually, evidence accumulates daily from research centers around the world supporting the idea that social anxiety is, in part, a complex manifestation of neurobiology. What does this mean?

Scientists have proposed that deep within our brain lies a complex, inborn "anxiety circuit." This anxiety circuit is nature's way of ensuring our survival. From an evolutionary perspective, we're programmed to register fear—and to act on it. In fact, the fear circuits in our bodies are some of the most highly developed. Nature's biggest concern is safety and survival, not whether we're enjoying ourselves in the process.

The anxiety circuit gives the brain's messengers—the neurotransmitters—several pathways to travel. For the socially anxious who, studies show, may have dysfunctions in their neurotransmitter systems, this means a ready-made path for producing anxiety-ridden reactions. Some studies have even found anatomical differences in the brains of individuals with social anxiety disorder. This research is still quite new, but with regular advances in technology, it shouldn't be long before more definitive statements can be made.

TEMPERAMENT. Another area of research closely tied to the causes of social anxiety is temperament. Temperament is defined as one's innate, inborn tendency to experience and respond to the environment in a characteristic manner. Think of it as a style of interacting with the world. For example, a toddler with an active temperament would have a great deal of energy, always be on the go, perhaps need less sleep, and so on.

The aspect of temperament we're concerned with is called "behavioral inhibition." This refers to the tendency to be cautious and watchful, especially in unfamiliar circumstances. It's like a checking system. When you're confronted with a situation, you stop and check to see if everything seems the way you expect it to be. If something appears awry, you're likely to move away from the situation. For example, a child with a strong behavioral inhibition system becomes uncomfortable when discovering a substitute teacher in the classroom. The child may stand frozen, appearing unsure of what to do.

Jerome Kagan, a psychologist at Harvard University, has contributed much to our understanding of behavioral inhibition in children. He monitored the development of twenty-two children with this trait as well as nineteen children who seemed uninhibited, and found many differences between these two groups of children. When confronted with stressful situations, children with behavioral inhibition

- show increased heart rates
- demonstrate greater muscular tension
- experience tension in their vocal cords
- contain higher levels of epinephrine, a substance that puts the brain on alert
- display higher levels of cortisol, a hormone present when one is under a constant state of apprehension

Some of the children Kagan followed are now adolescents. He found that those who were behaviorally inhibited as young children were more likely to develop social anxiety disorder in early adolescence. Although it seems likely that temperament can predispose someone to social anxiety, as with the other factors we've discussed, it's not enough alone to cause the problems.

There is another interesting physical marker of behavioral inhibition—blue eyes. Among Caucasian children, a "shy" temperament is more common in children with blue eyes. Although the exact mechanisms are not clear, iris pigmentation is associated with the concentration of certain neurotransmitters, and this may account for the connection between the two.

Keep in mind that behavioral inhibition is not all bad. We need some people in the world who don't impulsively jump into every situation that's presented. In fact, the psychologist Elaine Aronson finds the term "behavioral inhibition" too negative. She prefers the phrase "highly sensitive" to describe people who are thoughtful, cautious, and reserved.

BACK TO HOPE. As I told Mr. and Mrs. Longwell about this research, I noticed them relax. They listened intently and asked pertinent questions. Something seemed to click. Learning that there was a physical basis for Hope's anxiety freed them from thinking they were failures as parents. It also gave them hope. There was something else they hadn't yet tried that might give her the chance to be a happier child.

Hope responded well to the medication her doctor prescribed. The medicine, along with several "booster sessions" of therapy, left her well on her way toward living a life free from crippling fear. You can read more about the medications commonly used to treat social anxiety in Appendix A.

Life experience: The role of learning in social anxiety.
You may have heard it said that "biology isn't destiny." This means that even though our biological makeup exerts a strong influence on our development, it's not the whole story. Our environment also shapes us into the people we become. In this section, we look at three important ways life experience impacts the development of social anxiety: humiliating experiences, parenting styles, and observational learning.

HUMILIATING EXPERIENCES. Many people with social anxiety disorder recall a specific traumatic event associated with the beginning of their problems. A study conducted in 1985 by Professor Lars-Goran Öst at Stockholm University found that 58 percent of people with social phobia attributed the onset of their disorder to a traumatic experience. Other studies have replicated these findings. Dominic fits this pattern well.

When Dominic described the history of his social phobia, he traced his fears to an event that happened in fifth grade. Once when he wasn't paying attention in class, the teacher called on him to read aloud. He didn't know where they were in the story, so he guessed. When the whole class erupted in laughter, he knew he'd made a mistake. The girl in the desk behind him whispered where to begin reading, but by this time he was completely embarrassed—there was no way he could gain his composure. He tried to read, but he choked and mispronounced some words.

The next day, he paid closer attention. When he was called on to read, his throat tightened and his mouth felt like it was full of cotton. He asked to be excused to get a drink of water. While in the hallway, he heard laughing. He assumed the kids were making fun of him. From that point on, Dominic was afraid to read out loud. He worried so much about losing his place that he often had trouble concentrating. He continued to experience the sensation of choking. He tried clearing his throat, but it didn't help. Before long, his fear of reading generalized into a fear of speaking to the class at other times. Several weeks later, before giving an oral report, Dominic felt so sick he went into the bathroom and vomited.

Another type of traumatic experience is bullying. Leslie remembers being shy but not at all unhappy during elementary school. She had several friends and did well academically. In middle school, however, things began to change. A number of "tough kids" who had gone to different elementary schools began teasing her and bullying her. They said things like, "Why are you so shy?" and "Don't you know how to talk, little baby?"

Leslie didn't know how to defend herself. Despite feeling angry inside, she couldn't speak. She'd heard rumors that these were the kind of kids who would beat you up in the bathroom if you simply looked at them the wrong way. Leslie tried to become invisible so that others wouldn't notice her or pick on her. Unfortunately, the more she tried to avoid these bullies, the more they sought her out. Leslie later articulated that they must have perceived her as vulnerable—an easy target. She believes her shyness might not have developed into an anxiety disorder if it hadn't been for those negative experiences that year.

For Dominic and Leslie, a specific few events or a discrete period of time stands out in their minds as being significant. For other people, though, a series of smaller experiences can "prime the pump" for social anxiety to develop at a later point.

Remember, too, that interactions occur between your child's life experiences and his or her biological constitution. Research shows that traumatic experiences can actually alter the brain. For example, the humiliating experiences Dominic and Leslie endured may have contributed to the disruption of their neurotransmitter systems. This may be especially true if they were predisposed to social anxiety in other ways, such as being temperamentally shy and inhibited.

PARENTING STYLES. The way children are raised can play a role in the development of their social fears. This discussion is not meant to place blame. Most parents are well-meaning, and any child-rearing "mistakes" are not intentional. Still, it's an area that deserves attention.

Elena credits a large part of her social anxiety to her parents limiting her opportunities to develop relationships outside of the family. Her parents, of Mexican descent, worked hard to make a modest living for Elena and her three brothers. Her mother worked as a maid in a local motel; her father worked in a factory. They lived in a quiet neighborhood of small, neatly kept homes. Just down the street were larger, more stately homes. The public school Elena and her brothers attended was right around the corner.

Elena remembers the exact point when she gave up on having friends. It was a beautiful, crisp fall day with the smell of burning leaves in the air. Elena sat on her front steps, the breeze blowing her long, dark bangs off her forehead. She was waiting for her mother to come home from work. She had something exciting to tell her: Jennifer, a girl who lived down the street, had invited her to a slumber party that weekend. Jennifer had been nice to her since Elena and her family moved into the neighborhood, but this was the first time she'd been asked to do something with her outside of school.

When the bus let her mom off at the corner, Elena dashed down to the street to meet her. Before she could even finish telling her mom the news, her mom let loose a litany of negative comments: "That Jennifer's family is not our kind. They think they're too good for us, the way they drive that brand-new minivan and dress in those designer clothes. I don't see why she invited you to her stupid party anyway. You don't fit in with her crowd. Of course, you're not thinking of going, are you? . . ."

Elena's story illustrates some salient points about how parenting can influence the development of social anxiety. Elena's mother was prone to shyness and anxiety herself, but she often veiled it in irritability. Allowing Elena to attend the slumber party would mean she'd have to face some of her own fears and insecurities.

Research shows that socially anxious parents tend to restrict their children's opportunities for interaction with others. While it's probably not a conscious decision—most parents want the best for their children—it's easy to understand. Especially when children are young, it's often the mother who arranges playdates. At the very least, this means initiating a phone call. It might also mean making small talk with the other mom, even spending some time with her. In short, facilitating and allowing your child to socialize usually means you have to socialize as well.

Although it's tempting to avoid the distress altogether, the consequences are great. Social skills, like any other skill, are learned through practice. When children and adolescents don't enjoy numerous and varied opportunities to engage in social activities, their confidence naturally falters. Even adults need to season their social skills to remain comfortable and at ease around other people.

OTHER TYPES OF LEARNING. There are several other ways learning may play a role in the development of a child's social anxiety. In *vicarious learning,* also called *observational learning,* one acquires fear not through direct experience but indirectly, through watching others. Many animal studies have examined this process. For example, monkeys that watch other monkeys behave fearfully around snakes develop this same fear very quickly. Research conducted by Lars-Goran Öst found that 13 percent of people with social phobia identified observational learning as being an important factor in the onset of their disorder.

Remember, we've already shown that anxiety runs in families. Although part of this may be genetic, it's also easy to imagine how learning is involved. If you're already predisposed to anxiety and then witness a relative behaving anxiously and avoiding social situations, you'll naturally start to wonder if there is really something to fear. Perhaps you'll also begin to imitate the family member's behavior.

Observational learning doesn't have to occur within families. Witnessing someone else endure an embarrassing situation can lead you to worry about something similar happening to you.

When Allison was in the fourth grade, another girl in the class vomited all over herself, her desk, and much of the floor around her. Of course, many of the students in the class were yelling things such as "gross" and "disgusting." Although the teacher handled the situation well, this event greatly affected Allison. She thought she would never recover if something so humiliating as vomiting in public happened to her.

From that point on, Allison became extremely sensitized to any feelings of nausea. This was particularly a problem after lunch, so she began eating less and less at school. She was hungry in the afternoon and had trouble concentrating on her work, but she didn't want to risk eating something that would make her sick to her stomach. As is often the case, Allison's fears multiplied. She went from being afraid of vomiting at school to being afraid of any situation in which she would be the center of attention.

TAKING STOCK: WHAT FACTORS PLAYED A ROLE IN YOUR CHILD'S SOCIAL ANXIETY?

BELOW ARE SOME questions for you to answer. The first group deals with possible biological contributions to your child's social anxiety. The second group covers environmental factors. Going through this exercise may simply confirm what you already know, or it may reveal some new insights. The questions are in a yes/no format, but feel free to make comments alongside your answers.

One or more of our family members are shy.

❏ Yes
❏ No

One or more of our family members are the "nervous type."

❏ Yes
❏ No

Teachers or others describe my child as being shy and quiet, and/or I notice that my child is shy and quiet.

❏ Yes
❏ No

My child is typically cautious and reserved when entering new situations.

❏ Yes
❏ No

My child has always seemed very sensitive and reactive. For example, he or she was fussy as a baby and/or is more emotional than my other children or other children I know.

❑ Yes
❑ No

My child has blue eyes.

❑ Yes
❑ No

The more of the above items that you checked yes, the more likely there is a biological basis to your child's social anxiety.

There have been one or more times when my child was extremely embarrassed or humiliated.

❑ Yes
❑ No

My child witnessed someone else being embarrassed or humiliated, and this event greatly affected him or her.

❑ Yes
❑ No

My child has few opportunities for social interaction.

❑ Yes
❑ No

I (or my spouse) tend to be overprotective of my child.

❏ Yes
❏ No

The more of these items that you checked yes, the more likely that there is an environmental basis to your child's social anxiety.

Now take a few minutes to review your answers. Do you notice a pattern? Are your yes responses clustered primarily in the biology group? Or did you mark more items related to your environment? Remember, it's unlikely that one factor alone caused your child's social anxiety. Still, some people can determine the relative importance of contributing factors. For example, if Hope's parents answered these questions, they'd have answered yes to every item in the biology section except for the one about blue eyes.

The bottom line: You don't have to know *exactly* what caused your child's social anxiety problem to solve it. Sure, it's helpful to have some general ideas about how it developed, and by now you probably do. But it's not absolutely necessary.

WHY NOW? THE STRESS FACTOR

HERE WE LOOK at the question of timing. Why does social anxiety develop when it does? Why does it ebb and flow in its severity? Stress, it seems, is a huge factor.

In some cases, individuals are predisposed to anxiety problems but don't develop a full-blown disorder until stress overwhelms them. Adam was a quiet child who did well in school and had several close friends. He got along well with his parents and participated in a youth group at his church. His world was disrupted, however, when his father's company relocated and the family moved across the country. During January of his junior year of high school, Adam had to start all over making friends.

His parents thought he was handling the adjustment fairly well, but they'd been so caught up in the move that they hadn't noticed his withdrawal. He'd become moody and irritable. He worried constantly about what the other kids were thinking about him. His new school was so big that no one made an effort to include him, and he had trouble initiating anything on his own.

Many kids in Adam's situation adjust in time. But because Adam already had a number of predisposing factors in his background—a positive family history for anxiety and a quiet, shy temperament—he didn't adjust. Instead, his anxiety spiraled out of control. It wasn't until he failed his first semester in college that his parents realized the extent of his problems.

Stress can also explain why someone who has recovered from social anxiety disorder may experience a setback. Seventeen-year-old Becky had been on medication to treat her social anxiety for about a year and had participated in psychotherapy. During this time, Becky made huge strides in overcoming her fears. She'd joined some clubs at school, made some new friends, and even started dating. Things changed dramatically, however, when her mother was diagnosed with cancer. The stress of the situation took its toll and Becky reverted to her old pattern of avoiding practically all social contact. She isolated herself at a time when she most needed others' support.

Think back over your child's life. How has stress played a role in the course of his or her social anxiety?

WHAT MAINTAINS SOCIAL ANXIETY
ONCE IT STARTS?

SO FAR WE'VE looked at possible causes, or predisposing factors, of social anxiety, and we've shown how stress can set it off. Now let's explore what maintains social anxiety. Why doesn't your child just "grow out of it"? Why doesn't it simply go away on its own? After all, a certain percentage of people with depression improve without treatment. In contrast, such spontaneous remission rarely happens in cases of social anxiety disorder. Why does the fear of disapproval tend to be so chronic and unrelenting?

Avoiding isn't the answer. With any type of phobia, avoidance is a defining feature. People who are afraid of heights avoid top floors of buildings. People who are afraid of flying don't travel by plane. People who are afraid of driving on highways take the back roads. Avoidance is the automatic reaction to fear. And the immediate reduction in anxiety is a huge payoff. But it's certainly not the best long-term answer to the problem.

Avoidance maintains anxiety, even makes it worse, for several reasons. First, avoidance prevents a process called habituation from taking place. With habituation, your body becomes accustomed to a certain situation—it learns not to react so strongly. Habituation takes place only with repeated exposure, or contact, with the feared situation. So if you practice avoidance, your body doesn't have a chance to calm down, to learn on a physical level that it's not in danger. Second, avoidance prevents your thinking patterns from changing. When you avoid something you fear, you don't learn that you'd survive, and maybe even thrive. Finally, avoidance lowers your self-esteem. Over time, as you continually avoid situations, you begin to lose your confidence and feel like a failure.

We lead you through the step-by-step process you can take to help your child overcome avoidance in Chapter 7.

Thinking can cause more trouble. Faulty thinking patterns also keep many people stuck in the anxiety spiral. People with social anxiety disorder make two fundamental errors in the way they think about social or performance situations. These errors are called *probability* and *severity distortions*.

Probability distortions involve overestimating the likelihood that something will go wrong and people will judge you negatively. Some examples:

- I'm sure everyone will notice that my face is red when I have to introduce myself on the first day of class. They'll think I'm strange.
- People will see how nervous I am when I give the report in class and they'll think I don't know what I'm talking about.

Thoughts such as these come automatically when kids are anxious, and they seem perfectly logical at the time. Although it's possible other kids will judge harshly or tease, it's not as likely as your child thinks. Other kids have a lot on their minds and may not even notice that your child is blushing or nervous. Who knows? They may be worrying about their own performance. Still, nagging questions remain. What if they notice? What if they think I'm "strange"?

The big "what if" questions lead to severity distortions, which see receiving criticism or disapproval as a catastrophe. Consider these examples:

- When people see me blush, they'll think I'm dumb. No one will want to have anything to do with me. I won't have any friends.
- When my classmates notice how nervous I am, they'll laugh at me. I can't stand to have people make fun of me. I'll start to cry, and everyone will know I'm a loser.

We all want people to like us, and it's natural for children to want other kids to like them. But even if people disapprove of us sometimes, the consequences usually aren't as horrible as imagined. In Chapter 6, we go over in depth how you can help your child change these destructive thought patterns.

Worrying makes it worse. Worry is a major issue for children with social anxiety disorder and one of the more challenging aspects to conquer. It's another important part of what maintains social anxiety.

Worry involves projecting fear into the future. It's that barrage of "what if" questions and the associated anticipation and dread of something dire happening. People with social anxiety disorder worry about social events for weeks, even months, before they take place. While this heightened anxiety could be a plus if it led to useful preparation (for example, practicing for an upcoming piano recital), it's usually unproductive. More typical is that all of this worry leads to procrastination—and to even more worry.

Worry also keeps your body in a constant state of physical tension. Your neck may feel tense. You may have more headaches than usual. Perhaps you can't sleep well. The increased tension from worrying makes it more likely you'll suffer from the acute physical symptoms of anxiety when the actual event occurs. Because you're already like a stretched rubber band, it doesn't take nearly as much to make you pop. In addition, the constant state of tension leads your thoughts in negative directions, and you're more likely to make the probability and severity errors we discussed earlier.

Why is worry so difficult to overcome? In part, it's because of the superstitious quality of worrying. Somehow you think that if you worry enough, you can prevent something horrible from happening. And if nothing terrible occurs, the idea that worrying did help is reinforced. Or you think to yourself, "It was just luck. Next time I will probably screw up." Kids are already naturally prone to superstitious thinking, so this is a particular problem for them.

Paying attention (to the wrong things) can backfire. Another important element in the social anxiety spiral is one's focus of attention. This is a relatively newer area that's described by the psychologist Ronald Rapee in his book *Social Phobia: Clinical Applications of Evidence-Based Psychotherapy.*

According to Rapee, when socially anxious people enter a situation that they perceive as potentially threatening, their attention goes in two directions. First, they focus on a picture in their mind, a mental image, of how they believe they appear to others. This picture is usually inaccurate and distorted. At the same time, socially anxious people scan the "audience," the people around them, for any indication of disapproval. Because they're looking for negative feedback, they usually find it. Or they see disapproval when it's not really there. This negative feedback then reinforces their distorted internal snapshot and further exaggerates it. Let's look at this process in action.

Larry was an exceptionally bright high school student who excelled in science and math. He was taking tough advanced placement classes, working toward gaining admission to a prestigious college. Larry signed up to participate in a science fair. He thought it would be fun, plus it would look good on his college applications. He hadn't imagined, however, how frightening it would be to present his findings to the group of judges.

The day of the fair, Larry was so nervous he felt sick to his stomach. This had turned into a bigger deal than he realized. He was going to have to make a formal presentation not only to the judges but also to the other participants who would be observing.

The room was large, and it was set up with a podium and a microphone on a stage. Larry thought his voice sounded weird as he spoke into the microphone. He couldn't remember a thing, so he had to read from his notes. When he tried to flip through his note cards, his hands shook as if they had a life of their own. As the first few minutes (they seemed like hours) went on like this, he began forming a picture in his mind of how he must appear. He imagined his hands as huge and clumsy, even grotesque, while the rest of his body looked stiff and lifeless. As he focused on this image, he was sure the judges and other students could see him shake.

Larry noticed some of the students in the back talking to one another. "They must think my project is really lame," he thought. Larry was convinced he wouldn't do well in the competition.

Larry's anxiety prevented him from focusing on the task at hand. He wasn't able to present his findings for the science project that he knew inside and out. He was too focused on his hands and what the judges and other students were thinking of him.

Low mood exacerbates the situation. Mood is a final factor to consider in the social anxiety cycle. When your child is in a cheery mood, he's able to do more things socially and with more comfort than usual. His good mood might simply be because of a sunny day or the approaching weekend. Whatever the reason, he's generally more outgoing on days when things are going well.

The reverse may also be true. When he's feeling down in the dumps, he may be more likely to hide out in the house, not wanting to go outside and play with friends.

Clients frequently tell us they have "good days" and "bad days." While to some extent this is true for everyone, the consequences for people trying to overcome anxiety are greater. When people believe they can perform socially only when all conditions are good, they limit their opportunities.

Many of the techniques in this book can help your child with his or her moods as well as anxiety. Keep in mind, though, if your child is in a gloomy mood more days than not for several weeks, he might be suffering from clinical depression. If this is the case, talk to your doctor right away.

PUTTING IT ALL TOGETHER

THIS MODEL OF the development and maintenance of social anxiety is a lot of information to digest at one time. To briefly review, refer to "A Model of Social Anxiety" on page 43. In the boxes are the factors that increase one's vulnerability to social anxiety—the biological and the environmental contributions. The arrows between these factors indicate that they interact with one another. For example, we mentioned that traumatic experiences can lead to biochemical changes in the brain.

In the middle of the diagram is "The Stress Factor." If you're predisposed to social anxiety, stressful life events can propel you into the social anxiety spiral. We described Adam, who developed social anxiety after a stressful time when he had to change schools. Stress can also make symptoms of anxiety fluctuate over time. Remember Becky who had a major setback with her social anxiety following her mother's diagnosis of cancer.

At the bottom are the maintaining factors we discussed: avoidance, thinking errors, worry, attention problems, and mood. These factors overlap some, and they tend to play off of one another. For example, when your child's mood is low, she's more likely to worry and avoid. And then the more she worries and avoids, the lower her mood drops.

Because of this downward spiraling effect, overcoming social anxiety disorder certainly requires a lot of concerted effort. But teaching your child the latest breakthrough methods can help tremendously, and that's the subject of the rest of the book. In the following chapters, you'll see that your child isn't destined to be painfully shy forever as we show you step-by-step how to help your child triumph over fear. In short, you'll learn to be your child's greatest coach—not only nurturing her to develop her potential but also encouraging her to feel good about herself in the process.

A MODEL OF SOCIAL ANXIETY
Factors that can make someone vulnerable to social anxiety:

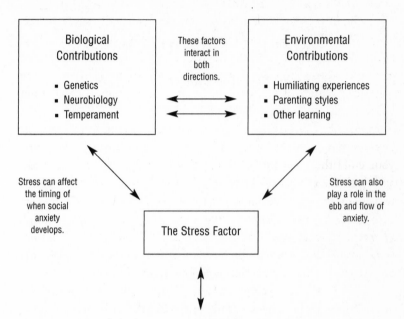

Factors that play a role in maintaining social anxiety once it begins:

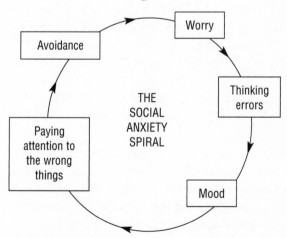

||||||||||||||||||||||||||||||||||||||||||||||||||||||||||||||||||||||||||||||

CHAPTER 3

Laying the Foundation

Seven Building Blocks for Success

B Y NOW you understand what social anxiety disorder is, what it looks like in children, and what factors contribute to its development and maintenance. Next we present seven important principles, or building blocks, that lay a strong foundation for the work to come. Think of these principles as a framework from which to begin—a mental mind-set to carry with you as you and your child progress through this book. Some of this material may seem a bit philosophical, but stick with it. We'll show you the practical importance of these principles throughout the chapter.

BUILDING BLOCK #1: START FROM A POSITION OF ACCEPTANCE

ACCEPTANCE IS DIFFICULT to explain, but once people experience its power firsthand, they understand why it's a necessary and important step in overcoming any problem. In fact, we think acceptance is so important that we've written about it in each of our previous books. The noted psychologist Marsha Linehan has written extensively about acceptance and how it's crucial to include in any type of "change" program. We like her statement, "Acceptance is the only way out of hell." By the time you finish reading this section, we believe you'll understand its significance. Let's first talk about what acceptance involves.

Acceptance is an attitude. Acceptance is a way of looking at ourselves and the world around us. It implies a willingness and an openness to see things as they truly are, without judgment. For example, as we wrote in *Painfully Shy,* if you're feeling anxious, you're feeling anxious. That's all. It doesn't mean it's horrible or catastrophic.

It doesn't mean the anxiety will last forever. It doesn't mean that you won't be able to handle it. It doesn't mean anything except that you're feeling anxious at a particular moment.

We're often so busy putting things into categories—"this is good" or "this is bad"—that we miss the actual experience of the moment. Certainly, it doesn't come naturally to suspend judgment, tolerate uncertainty, and turn off the ongoing internal commentary that plays in our minds. But that's what's needed, because all any of us can truly know is what's happening right here, right now.

Acceptance doesn't equal approval. Many people think that acceptance means approval, and this confusion causes people to balk at the whole idea. In the way we're discussing it, however, these two aren't equivalent. For example, accepting the fact that there is poverty in the world doesn't mean you approve of poverty.

Acceptance also doesn't mean you're giving up. Accepting your doctor's diagnosis of cancer, for example, doesn't mean you'll refuse treatment and just roll over and die. In addition, acceptance doesn't preclude taking action. Once you learn your child has social anxiety disorder, you're not going to stop there and tell yourself there's nothing you can do. Acceptance is simply paying attention to the way things are and then taking the next appropriate step.

Acceptance alleviates suffering. Perhaps the greatest benefit of learning the art of acceptance is that it alleviates unnecessary suffering. We're not saying that you won't feel any more pain—you will. But the kind of acceptance we're talking about can lead you to peace amid the pain, calm in the center of chaos, serenity in spite of suffering. Does this sound too good to be true?

Here's a personal example of how acceptance helped us transcend suffering. Although the story in itself isn't about social anxiety, it poignantly illustrates how acceptance works in the real world.

For the first three years of our son Jesse's life, he had a multitude of health problems. One of our major concerns was his chronic vomiting. When he was an infant, our pediatrician reassured us that his spitting up was normal. Since this was our first child, we had no way to compare how much or how often was normal. We had an inkling that his vomiting was somewhat unusual when we saw others' horrified reactions as they witnessed the event. When we began introducing solid foods, we hoped the vomiting would stop. Unfortunately, the situation grew worse. Jesse stopped gaining weight at nine months and started losing weight about the time of his first birthday.

Overwrought with worry after a particularly difficult weekend, we decided the time had come (perhaps we'd waited too long) to change pediatricians. Our new pediatrician took the matter seriously, completed extensive testing, and made the diagnosis of gastroesophageal reflux. We hoped an end was near when Jesse began taking a medicine frequently prescribed to treat reflux. To our dismay, however, the first medicine didn't work. We tried many other medicines. None of them worked. He still vomited daily, often several times a day.

This wasn't the way we'd envisioned our life with our firstborn child. In addition to our worry about his physical health, this problem greatly diminished our quality of life. It was a major challenge getting ready in the morning. Many times we'd be walking out the door when Jesse would vomit on himself and on at least one of us, sending us back to the bathtub. More than once he threw up on the dog. We didn't go out much—it's hard to find a babysitter willing to deal with this situation. We stayed awake all night listening for sounds of vomiting (he often did it when he was in bed). We spent hours and hours theorizing about what was wrong with him. We went to medical libraries and read anything that might apply.

During one office visit, the doctor spent a lot of time with us and gave us a good heart-to-heart talk. He told us that we had to accept Jesse's vomiting—we should stop fighting it. It wasn't life threatening at this point, he said; Jesse's weight had stabilized. The only thing to do was wait until he outgrew the problem. This wasn't what we wanted to hear. We wanted the problem fixed, solved, ended. How could we go on dealing with a child who vomited daily? Somehow, though, the doctor's message of acceptance sank in. We realized we weren't being fair to ourselves or to Jesse. We had restricted our life too much. The doctor was right. We had to start living, in spite of the vomiting.

What did acceptance involve for us? First, it meant grieving. We cried. We allowed ourselves to feel sad. As much as we'd tried to gain control of the problem, it was out of our control. Next, we "let go" of trying to prevent the vomiting. If he was going to vomit, so be it. We started getting out of the house more, carrying a bucket and a change of clothes wherever we went. We praised each other when we handled a tough situation. For example, we vividly remember the rainy Halloween night when he started to vomit while trick-or-treating at the shopping mall—how we quickly dumped the candy he had already collected onto the floor so the pumpkin-shaped bucket would be "available." We laughed about our situation a bit more. We impressed ourselves with our ability to clean up vomit one minute and eat dinner the next. We supported each other and sought support from friends and family whenever possible.

As we accepted the situation, little by little, our suffering diminished. We handled things better, we enjoyed Jesse more, we were more relaxed. This attitude of acceptance carried with it other benefits: Our thinking gained clarity, and we trusted ourselves more. We knew it could not be healthy for anyone, much less someone so young, to vomit so much. Another year and a half had passed and he'd still not outgrown the problem. When we asked our pediatrician for a consultation, he continued to assert that it probably wasn't a big deal and even suggested that we might have "conditioned" Jesse to vomit. The doctor nonetheless referred us to a pediatric gastroenterologist for another opinion. After another round of more invasive tests, the specialist found nothing conclusive. Next, we saw a psychologist who specialized in working with children and their parents. Was it possible the doctor was right, that we'd subtly reinforced our son's vomiting? The psychologist didn't think so, and she encouraged us to continue seeking medical answers.

Two weeks after his third birthday, Jesse was awake all night coughing and vomiting. When we took him to the doctor's office the next morning, we saw an associate of our regular pediatrician. She noticed that Jesse was having difficulty breathing and hospitalized him. The next morning, the same doctor visited us in his room. She said, "I reviewed Jesse's chart from front to back, and I believe I know what's wrong with him. He has asthma and probably severe allergies." Looking back on it now, we're amazed that no one had mentioned this as a possibility to us before. In fact, one of the theories we'd developed ourselves had to do with allergies, but Jesse's first pediatrician saw no validity in it. Jesse received intensive treatment for his asthma while in the hospital, and he continued to take breathing treatments daily for the next several years. He's doing much better now, vomiting only rarely when his asthma or allergies flare up.

As you can see, acceptance doesn't come quickly or easily. It's a process, much as grieving someone's death is a process. Only after you go through the shock, the denial, the anger, and the despair can you move forward with a spirit of patience and trust. Practicing the art of acceptance taught us to seek answers while at the same time tolerating uncertainty. We couldn't control what was happening in Jesse's body. We couldn't force the medical professionals to take us seriously. We couldn't change or control any of the events. All we could do was to take charge, as best we could, of our reactions to those events.

What this means in practical terms. You may be thinking to yourself, "Okay, I understand the general idea of what you're talking about, but how does this apply to my situation?"

By now you probably have a good idea of what you're facing with your child. No doubt you've experienced feelings related to what we've described. Some parents are relieved to know their child has something with an actual name—a disorder that is now recognized by professionals and can be treated. Other parents are upset. They don't want to think their child isn't "normal" in any respect, much less might have a bona fide mental disorder. Some parents worry. What will this mean for my child? Will he or she lead a full, happy life? Most parents have a mixture of feelings, and these feelings likely vary from time to time. Rest assured, all your feelings are normal, so don't beat up on yourself if you're having a hard time.

Acceptance in this context means several things:

- Accepting your own feelings as okay and normal.
- Allowing yourself to feel the full range of your feelings.
- Accepting that your child has problems with shyness and/or social anxiety, but realizing that this is only one aspect of your child and does not take away from his or her unique strengths or inherent worth.
- Accepting your child for who she is. You're not likely to change her into an outgoing, social butterfly—and we wouldn't necessarily want that to happen. There are some hidden strengths in being shy.
- Assuring your child that you love him just as he is. At the same time, finding that delicate balance of letting him know you're available to help him "stretch"—to try new things and to reach any goals he wants to pursue.

Below are some questions for you to answer. Take your time, and remember that there are no right or wrong answers. By pondering these questions, you're taking an important step in the process of acceptance.

It may seem like a contradiction, but only by starting from a position of acceptance can you help your child grow, develop, and change.

QUESTIONS FOR THOUGHT

1. Before your child was born, did you have a vision of what his or her personality would be like? What did you hope for?

2. In what ways is your child's personality like or not like what you had envisioned?

3. Have you allowed yourself to grieve any disappointments you feel?

4. How have your child's personality characteristics been advantageous? (For example, shy children aren't as likely to get into trouble in school.)

5. How do you express your acceptance of your child?

BUILDING BLOCK #2: SEPARATE YOUR OWN ISSUES FROM YOUR CHILD'S

ANOTHER DIFFICULT BUT important task is to separate your own issues from those of your child. As we discussed in Chapter 2, anxiety can run in families. It's possible that not only does your child have social anxiety disorder, but you do as well. Many parents have said that the only thing more difficult than struggling with social anxiety is watching their child struggle with it.

Rachel certainly felt this way. She had grown up painfully shy and had developed a full-blown anxiety disorder in college. Despite having been awarded an academic scholarship, Rachel faltered in her classes.

She was terrified of having to speak in front of a group, and to her dismay, almost all her classes involved some type of public speaking. Her anxiety built to the point that she frequently skipped her classes. Before the end of the first semester, Rachel had dropped out of school and moved home. She got a job as a receptionist in a law office, a position that was certainly beneath her potential. She eventually married and had two children, Dana and Sam. When I met Rachel, her daughter was in the second grade and her son was eighteen months old.

Rachel described her daughter as shy and cautious. Dana apparently had a difficult time making friends and sometimes came home saying, "No one likes me." Similarly, Rachel's son hid behind her when they were around new people, and he cried each time she left him with a babysitter, even a familiar one.

"I am terrified of history repeating itself," Rachel said. "I die inside every day thinking that my children will someday be as miserable as I was."

I understood Rachel's concerns. Her social anxiety had contributed to much despair in her life, and she naturally didn't want her children to endure the same pain.

Some of Rachel's concern was misguided, however. She focused on every aspect of her children's lives that could signal a possible problem. While many young children experience stranger anxiety and distress at separating from their mothers, Rachel was convinced this meant that her toddler, Sam, was destined to a life crippled by social fears. She was also obsessed with her daughter's "social life." Every day after school she questioned Dana about how recess had gone, whom she played with, which girls talked to her, whom she ate lunch with, and so on. As you might imagine, Dana sometimes felt interrogated by her mother, and she definitely got the message loud and clear that it was important to her mother that she be popular.

Perhaps you don't have social anxiety but some other anxiety problem, or perhaps you've wrestled with depression. Whatever the case, all of us have been through tough times in our lives, and it's easy to assume we know what our child is feeling because we've been through something similar. However, these assumptions may or may not be correct.

Jeremy, who had always been heavy and picked on as a child, once observed his son on the playground and noticed that he was shooting basketballs by himself. His heart sank. "Poor guy. I know just how he feels. It's miserable to be ostracized by the other kids," he thought to himself.

That evening, he asked his son about it. Contrary to what he had imagined, his son was enjoying himself and doing what he had chosen to do. "I played kickball with the other kids for a while, but I felt like practicing my free throws," his son explained. "I was happy when no one was playing basketball so I could have the hoop all to myself."

Of course, a parent who knows his child well often makes correct assumptions about how the child is feeling. Just be careful not to go too far and think that you're *always* right. Check things out with your child, and recognize when your reactions may be stemming from your own experiences.

It also might help to remind yourself that professionals' understanding and ability to treat social anxiety disorder and its potential complications are much more sophisticated than when you were growing up. This means that your child doesn't have to have the same experiences you did.

Below are some additional questions for you to ponder. Take your time, and again remember there are no right or wrong answers.

QUESTIONS FOR THOUGHT

1. Can you think of a time when you may have confused your issues with those of your child?

2. How did you react?

3. How did your reaction affect your child?

4. What could you have done differently?

BUILDING BLOCK #3: SUPPORT YOUR
CHILD BY LISTENING

WHEN WE TALK to couples, we place a great deal of emphasis on communication skills—particularly on how to listen. While it's obvious that communication (or lack thereof) can make or break a marriage, you may not realize that it's also critically important in how we parent our children. When we truly listen to our children, they feel valued and understood. They're more likely to have healthy self-esteem, and they're more likely to cooperate with us when we encourage them to take risks in overcoming their social anxiety.

In the past, listening was a revered and integral part of life. Neighbors sat on their front porches and talked, and extended family was typically nearby, available to lend an ear when needed. Televisions and video games didn't exist, and people spent more time simply being together and sharing stories. With our hectic lifestyles today, this kind of quality time typically doesn't happen without some concerted effort.

How do we know that listening is so important? Why should we make the time for it?

Research from many different disciplines points to listening as a crucial, even curative process. For example, psychotherapy "outcome" research examines the effectiveness of different types of therapy. Results from numerous experiments point out that the major ingredient responsible for determining whether positive change occurs is the quality of the helper-client relationship. In other words, a key factor in whether therapy works is whether you feel that your therapist is really listening. Similarly, medical research has found that cancer patients have better recovery rates if they perceive their oncologists as warm and understanding—good listeners.

The type of listening we're talking about is called *empathic* or *active* listening. It involves putting your own agenda on hold and trying instead to identify and understand what your child is saying. Here are some guidelines:

- While listening, try to put yourself in your child's shoes. Focus on what he or she is feeling, not just what is said.
- Accept your child's right to have his or her own thoughts and feelings.
- Demonstrate your acceptance through your posture, tone of voice, and facial expressions.
- While listening, try to avoid asking questions, expressing your own opinions, offering solutions, or making judgments.
- After your child has finished speaking, summarize and restate the most important thoughts and feelings that were expressed.

This type of listening may seem a bit awkward at first. Don't worry, though. It will feel more natural with practice. If your savvy child looks at you funny or questions you about what you're doing, it's fine to say something such as, "I've realized I may not always listen as well as I should, and I'm trying to do better."

For Rachel, the hardest part of listening to her daughter talk about problems at school was keeping her own emotional reactions in check. She told me about the first time Dana came home complaining about recess. "It was my worst nightmare hearing her say that no one played with her, that she went to the other side of the playground and played by herself. I thought I was going to break down and cry on the spot," Rachel explained.

Rachel did indeed have a difficult job. In order to support her daughter, she needed to put her own issues on hold. If she truly were to listen to Dana, she couldn't become consumed with her own thoughts, such as, "Oh, my God, I've cursed my child with this."

What can Rachel do? First, she needs to encourage Dana to talk more about it. She can say, "I'm glad you're talking to me about this. I want to hear more." Then Rachel can calmly listen, without offering advice or judgment at this point.

Depending on what Dana says, she can check out possible things she might be feeling. She can say, "It sounds like you felt lonely and sad playing by yourself." Or, "I wonder if you weren't sure how to join in with the other kids."

By listening and helping your child talk about feelings, you're taking away some of the sting and setting the stage for future problem solving.

We think active listening is so important that we recommend scheduling at least fifteen minutes a day (more is great) when you can focus exclusively on your child—not the dishes that need to be done or the bills that need to be paid. In her wonderful book *Worried No More,* Aureen Pinto Wagner, Ph.D., calls this *YAMA* time, or *You and Me Alone* time. It's a time to sit down and relax, chat or, as Dr. Wagner says, "yammer" about nothing in particular with your child. Try not to direct or control the conversation. Let your child take the lead.

Younger children especially love spending this time with you. Even older kids, who at first may think it's weird, will grow to count on this one-on-one time and even look forward to it. Find a consistent time that works for you and stick with it. Both you and your child will be richly rewarded.

Take some time to reflect on the following questions.

QUESTIONS FOR THOUGHT

1. Do I make time to listen to my child?

2. Do I allow her to simply talk, without offering my opinion?

3. Do I help my child identify his feelings?

4. What happens if I jump in too quickly with advice or suggestions?

BUILDING BLOCK #4: FOCUS ON THE POSITIVE

HAND IN HAND with active listening is the important task of focusing on the positive. Too often we forget that the best way to encourage our child is to use positive comments and sometimes even small rewards. Instead, it's all too easy to lapse into criticism and nagging.

Stephanie's ten-year-old daughter Danielle had problems initiating after-school activities with friends. She came home from school every day, did her homework, and watched television but complained about being lonely and bored. Stephanie admitted that at times Danielle annoyed her so much with her glum face and whining that she'd yell things such as, "Just go outside and play with the neighborhood kids" or, "You're driving me crazy."

Sometimes parents can become even more frustrated and make shameful comments about the child: "Why can't you be more outgoing like your brother," or, "You'll never have any friends if you sit around and play Nintendo all day." Keep in mind that shame never works to make your child less shy, and in fact, has the opposite effect.

Instead of using negative comments, the best way to shape new behavior is to notice and reward desired behavior consistently and frequently. And remember to start small in what you expect. Don't wait until your child is selected for the school talent show before you show your pride. For a child who rarely speaks to adults, making eye contact with the mail carrier may be quite an accomplishment.

What type of reinforcement works best? Often verbal praise is all that's needed. The praise should be specific to be most effective. For example, telling your child, "Good job!" is not nearly as powerful as saying, "I noticed how you waved and smiled at the neighbor. I bet that made her feel good."

In addition, young children often respond to sticker charts, and this is a fine way to establish a new behavior. For example, your child might receive a sticker every day he says hello to two people. Once the behavior has become a habit, you can phase out the stickers.

Too often, kids with anxiety receive a lot of attention for "meltdowns" or other behavioral components of their problem. This is a natural reaction. When your child has a tantrum just before going to a family reunion, for example, you have to deal with it. But unfortunately, the memory of what should have been a pleasurable event gets tarnished by the anxiety reaction.

William was expected to be part of the chorus in his elementary school's Christmas program. His parents had taken off work, and both sets of grandparents had made arrangements to attend. That morning, William refused to get dressed and go to school. He yelled and screamed at his parents that he wouldn't be in the program. This created a whole series of unpleasant events that, needless to say, put a damper on everyone's holiday spirit.

To counteract the negative interactions that may take place regarding your child's anxiety, try to build a bank of positive memories your child can draw on. Anxious kids frequently have trouble with situations that aren't predictable and routine. This means that the usual times for building photo-album-worthy memories, such as holidays, vacations, parties, and visits with relatives, can be fraught with tension and potential stress overload. Try to create other times in your family life when your child can feel special and a part of things.

Along with this, take an inventory of your child's strengths and look for ways to acknowledge these. Despite the fact that your child has difficulty in social situations, she has many other positive aspects to her personality. Does your child have a good sense of humor? Is she creative? You get the idea.

In addition, even the shy aspect of your child's personality likely has some positive benefits. For example, many shy children are thoughtful, self-controlled, conscientious, sensitive to other's needs and feelings, gentle, caring, and loving.

QUESTIONS FOR THOUGHT

1. What are my child's strengths?

2. How can I further nurture these strengths?

3. Do I offer my child frequent and specific praise?

4. Do I avoid making comparisons to other siblings or other children?

5. Do I avoid shaming comments?

BUILDING BLOCK #5: WATCH THE LABELS

ALTHOUGH "SHY" IS not a negative term in our minds, we realize that in our Western culture it's not generally considered a desirable trait. Bernardo Carducci, a nationally published researcher on shyness, frequently comments on our society's prejudice against shyness. He notes that our society places a greater value on being bold and outgoing (think Donald Trump), often ignoring the strengths of those who are more thoughtful and reserved. Think about it. When was the last time someone told you, "Wow! It's so great that your child is shy"?

In Elaine Aronson's book *The Highly Sensitive Person,* she describes some extremely important research dealing with this issue of culture. The study, conducted by Xinyin Chen and Kenneth Rubin of the University of Waterloo in Ontario, Canada, and Yuerong Sun of Shanghai Teachers University, compared children in both cities to determine what traits made children popular. Among the group of 480 students in Shanghai, "shy" and "sensitive" children were the most sought after as friends. In contrast, among the 296 Canadian children, shy and sensitive children were the least desirable. You can see, then, that whether children are accepted by others can have little to do with their personality and much to do with the prevailing cultural norms.

Because of our culture's view of shyness, it's a good idea to give your children other terms in which to think about themselves.

INSTEAD OF SAYING THIS:	TRY THIS:
"You're shy."	"You're talkative with people you know well.
"Don't be afraid."	"It takes a little while for you to feel comfortable with new people."
"You're anxious."	"You're cautious. You like to know what something is all about before you try it."

You might be thinking, "That's all well and good, but what about other people calling my child shy in front of her? I can't do anything about that."

Shari and Dave ran into this situation frequently with their daughter, Emily, who was three years old and naturally cautious around unfamiliar people. But they developed a method for dealing with others' comments. Whenever they were at church, someone would invariably ask Emily a question, and she wouldn't answer. If the person then asked, "Oh, she's shy, isn't she?" Dave and Shari made sure to say something like, "Wait until you get to know Emily. She'll talk to you about anything."

By reflecting on the questions below, you'll get in touch with your feelings about the label "shy."

QUESTIONS FOR THOUGHT

1. What comes to mind when I think of the word "shy"?

2. Do I try to avoid labeling my child?

3. Am I assertive with others when they try to label my child?

4. Do I give my child positive ways to reframe the label "shy"?

BUILDING BLOCK #6: GIVE IT TIME

ENCOURAGING A CAUTIOUS child takes a lot of time and patience, and it's best to give your child permission to go at his or her own pace.

Peggy seemed instinctively to know not to push four-year-old Tyler too quickly in new situations. Tyler had wanted to take gymnastics lessons for as long as she could remember. The first night of the class, however, he changed his mind. It was a struggle just to get him to the Y for the lessons, and then he didn't want to participate. He cried when the instructor tried to coax him into joining the other children; instead, he jumped into his mom's lap and grasped her neck so tightly she thought she might choke.

How did Peggy handle the situation? What did she do? Probably just as important as what she did, is what she didn't do. Peggy *didn't*

- tell her son not to cry
- tell him, "There's nothing to be scared about"
- tell him, "Don't be so shy"
- act angry and say, "You were the one who wanted to do this"

All of these responses are understandable from a parent who is frustrated and embarrassed, but they do nothing to help the situation and, in the long run, hurt the child's self-esteem.

Instead, here are some of the helpful things Peggy told her son:

- "It's okay to watch first."
- "You like to check things out before you jump right in."
- "New things are hard."
- "I used to feel scared when I tried new things."

By making these types of statements, she validated his concerns. In effect, she let him know his feelings were normal and nothing to be ashamed of.

When your child will be experiencing something new, talk at home about what to expect. If you've been to the Y, talk about what the building looks like, where the gymnastics room is located, and if any neighborhood children you know are also registered for the class. Plan to arrive early so your child can become more comfortable before the class begins—perhaps meet the teacher and see where you will be sitting.

Tyler needed to watch for most of the entire first class. Because his mom had told him this was okay and nothing to feel bad about, he loosened up and seemed to enjoy himself, even though he was mostly observing. Toward the end of the class, Peggy walked with him to where the group was, and they sat together on the floor while the teacher demonstrated how to do something. By allowing Tyler to go at his own pace, Peggy turned what could have been an unpleasant experience into a successful one—and one that he would feel comfortable trying again.

Here is another group of questions for you to answer. If you're not sure of a response to any item, that's okay. These aren't questions that you have to answer right away. You might need time to mull some of them over.

QUESTIONS FOR THOUGHT

1. When I try to push my child too hard and too fast, what result do I get?

2. How could I work on being more patient with my child? With myself?

3. Do I get embarrassed when my child doesn't join in like the other kids?

4. How can I reassure myself that differences are okay and that not every child has to be the life of the party?

BUILDING BLOCK #7: REALIZE YOU CAN'T PROTECT YOUR CHILD FROM ALL PAIN

IT'S NATURAL TO want to shield our children from adversity in life, but children must also learn—in small, gradual doses—to deal with reality.

If you're a sensitive person who has struggled with being painfully shy, this is probably the hardest lesson to take to heart. After all, you remember what it was like to feel sick to your stomach on show-and-tell days. You know how your heart raced when you were called on to answer a question in class. You felt the agony and the unfairness at not being invited to the popular kids' birthday parties. Of course you don't want this for your child. Realize, though, that to some extent there are normal "traumas" that children must go through. If you protect them from everything, they won't grow and mature as they should.

Not too long ago, our son, Jesse, started middle school. We were a bit anxious about how the transition would go from a small, neighborhood school where he knew almost everyone to a larger, more impersonal school halfway across town. One day early in the school year, Jesse came home with a bruise behind his knee. When I questioned him about it he told me that a boy had pushed him against one of the lunchroom tables. I was aghast and started asking a lot of questions about the incident. Jesse, however, took it in stride. He said, "Mom, I didn't take it personally. This kid picks on everyone." While I don't condone bullying, I realized that I could make a big deal out of this incident, or I could let Jesse learn the unfortunate lesson that not everyone in the world is nice.

Even parents who don't tend to be anxious themselves may overprotect their children. These parents are usually well-intentioned and motivated to spare their children from undue distress or embarrassment. For example, when a child struggles to find the words to answer someone's question, you might want to save him by jumping in and talking for him. Or when a child appears anxious before trying something new and begs not to go, you might think you're being kind by giving in and letting her stay home.

Sometimes it's not simply a case of trying to shield children from pain; it's often easier to give in and do something ourselves, even though we know we should encourage them to do it on their own. It takes a lot of effort to deal with an anxious child, especially if you're not familiar with the strategies we present in this book. But as the Swedish writer Ellen Key reminds us in *Words of Women— Quotations for Success,* we're not doing children any favor by being overprotective, for any reason. She poetically states, "At every step the child should be allowed to meet the real experience of life; the thorns should never be plucked from his roses."

On the next page is a final group of questions for you to answer.

QUESTIONS FOR THOUGHT

1. In what ways do I overprotect my child?

2. What lessons might my child be missing as a result?

3. How can I deal with my own feelings so I'm not quite so overprotective?

4. What small steps could I take in this area?

YOU DON'T HAVE TO BE PERFECT

THESE BUILDING BLOCKS, or principles, are certainly ideals worth striving for, but parents aren't perfect, and they don't need to be. Simply do your best to incorporate the ideas from this chapter into your consciousness and into your day-to-day routines. Accept your child. Don't try to make him into something he's not. Make time to listen to your child, and let her know you value her strengths. Watch your own reactions and try not to confuse your issues with your child's. Realize that the world can be both beautiful and harsh, and you can't protect your child from everything. Our best guess is that if you're reading this book, you're already a nurturing parent who, with a little guidance from us, can help your shy child shine.

||||||||||||||||||||||||||||||||||||||||||||||||||||||||||||||||||||||||||||||

CHAPTER 4

Making a Game Plan

Goal Setting with Your Child

I N T H E previous chapter, you learned some important, fundamental principles for parenting your shy, socially anxious child. You also reflected on your thoughts and feelings about shyness and how you interact with your child. Now that we've laid a strong foundation, it's time to get more specific. In this chapter, we show you how to develop a game plan for changing your child's behavior.

When we work with socially anxious adults, we ask them about their goals. We help them articulate what they want to be able to do and how they want to feel different in social situations. In doing so, we are helping them visualize how their life can be better.

Helping children with anxiety can be much trickier. Children are less able to put into words what they want to change. They may also have difficulty even recognizing that they're feeling anxious. Despite this, however, most kids know they want to feel better—they just don't know how to go about it. That's where you come in.

As a parent, you need to be like a good Little League coach. Sure, you want to win games, but your primary goal is to help the kids on the team have a good experience and develop their abilities. You want your kids to give their best effort. If they work hard and give their all, they have been a success, even if the scoreboard doesn't always reflect it.

Similarly, we want shy kids to be able to face anxiety-provoking situations and learn that they can survive—even thrive. We want them to develop confidence. We want them to learn that the very act of facing fear makes them successful.

Let's talk about how we do this.

TEAM-BUILDING

THE FIRST STEP is to get your child on the same team with you. You want your child, on some level, to agree that overcoming social anxiety is a worthwhile pursuit. Obviously, since you can't do the work for your child, you need to enlist his or her cooperation. As you read on, keep in mind the points we made in Chapter 3 about the power of acceptance. As you work to form a "team spirit" with your child, you need to walk a fine line between communicating acceptance ("You're okay as you are") and the desirability of change ("You can try new things").

Create motivation. As we've stated, children may not know why they're anxious. All they're sure of is they want to avoid—at all costs—whatever situation is triggering their anxiety. They may never realize what they are missing or giving up in the process. It's your job as a good coach to help your child understand the benefits of mastering his or her anxiety.

Talk with your child about what he or she has to gain: more friends, greater comfort in certain situations, perhaps fewer physical complaints, and enhanced feelings of self-confidence. It can help to write these things down on a list.

Benefits of Overcoming Social Anxiety

_____

_____

_____

_____

_____

_____

The more reasons and benefits you can generate with your child, the better. The work of confronting and mastering social anxiety can be challenging, and you want your child to realize that the pay-offs will be worth the effort.

You may meet with some initial resistance. Anxious kids by nature don't like anything new. Your child is likely to say, "I already have friends" or, "I'm fine." Your sensitive child may very well sense where this discussion is going. He may be fearful that you will ask him to do things he feels he cannot do. There may be shame in talking about the fear and anxiety, or there may be worry about disappointing you. Don't let this resistance throw you off course. Be low-key in your approach. You certainly want to keep this discussion upbeat. It may be helpful to have several shorter conversations rather than one long one so your child can get used to the ideas you're presenting.

Throughout all of this, remember to practice the empathic listening presented in the previous chapter. Don't lecture. Don't get into debates with your child about the benefits of overcoming social anxiety. Use your best communication skills to understand his or her concerns without buying into possible notions that the situation is hopeless or that nothing can change.

Lessening social anxiety: It's a lot like getting in physical shape. It can help to draw the analogy of overcoming social anxiety to getting in good physical shape. Everyone needs exercise to be healthy, and everyone needs some degree of social skill and comfort to function effectively in the world. So even if your child claims she doesn't need friends or she doesn't need to be able to speak in school, you know otherwise. We're not saying your child has to be the most popular kid in school, but he or she does need a certain level of basic "social fitness" to be healthy.

Getting in physical shape is a lot like getting in "social shape." You have to begin slowly or you'll develop sore muscles, become discouraged, and end up quitting. You also have to "work out" consistently, not just here and there. And if you take a few weeks off and do nothing, you quickly lose your tone. Star athletes must work out nearly every day, and most people, even those skilled at socializing, must routinely work out their "social muscles."

How can making this analogy help? First of all, it can give you, the parent and the coach, the motivation and patience to stick with the game plan. As a coach, you help your child learn new skills and encourage him to keep practicing. You continue to push your child to exercise his "social muscles." Keep in mind that any reluctance you encounter from your child is fear, and fear can be faced and conquered.

Second, this analogy may help you explain to your child some of the concepts we're presenting in an interesting and fun way. Most of the children we've worked with, both boys and girls, like the sports analogies and find them helpful.

In addition, the metaphor of "getting in shape" can normalize the process of dealing with social anxiety. Everyone has to work at social skills; this doesn't mean something is wrong with you. It's simply something you do to stay healthy, just like brushing your teeth.

Bribery isn't all bad. Our twelve-year-old son was listening intently as we discussed this chapter. We were talking about how we can motivate children to do things they may not want to do. He piped up, "You could always bribe them."

Well, Jesse had a point, and although we weren't sure about his choice of words, it's true that bribery isn't all bad. Most parents have gotten the message that you shouldn't "bribe" your children, but it's really just another way of talking about the behavioral principle of reinforcement.

Remember that in Chapter 3 we said you should focus on the positive. The concept of reinforcement is very similar. You try to shape desirable behavior by rewarding it. This doesn't mean you have to pay your child for doing something she's afraid of, but it does mean you may want to work out a system of incentives.

For young children, this may mean devising a sticker chart whereby they earn stickers for completing tasks related to overcoming their anxiety. Perhaps after earning a certain number of stickers they can rent a movie or choose a special meal for dinner one evening. For older kids, a point or token system whereby they earn time for video games or some other privilege typically works well.

Keep in mind, though, that verbal praise is always welcome; don't underestimate how important and valuable this can be to your child. Shy and anxious kids generally want to please, so knowing that you notice and appreciate their efforts goes a long way toward motivating them to continue.

SET YOUR SIGHTS ON A GOAL

AFTER YOU'VE MADE some progress in motivating your child, the next step is to define a goal. Having a goal answers the question, "What do I want my child to accomplish?" You might feel that the answer is obvious. "I want my child to be free of social anxiety." Of course, this is a desirable goal, but it is far too general to be very useful. A useful goal must be specific.

To help you determine a specific goal, ask yourself these questions, and of course involve your child in the discussion when appropriate:

- What type of social situation do I want my child to stop avoiding?
- How do I want my child to feel in that situation?

As you can see from these questions, a specific goal contains two components: The situation you want your child to handle better and how you want your child to feel in that situation.

Here are some examples of specific goals you might have for your child:

- I want my child to raise his hand in class with relative ease.
- I want my child to call a friend on the phone with minimal anxiety.
- I want my child to give a book report without undue anxiety.

Now that you have some examples, think about what goals you want to work on with your child and jot them down in the lines below. To help you in this process, go back to Chapter 1 and review your answers to the questionnaire, "Does My Child Have Social Anxiety Disorder?" Again, make sure the goals you list contain both the type of situation you want your child to master and how you want him or her to feel in that situation.

Possible Goals

_____

_____

_____

One important note about goals before we move on: They need to be realistic and achievable. Tackling social anxiety with unrealistic expectations leads to frustration and disappointment. For example, it is not realistic to expect to eliminate *all* anxiety in *all* situations. Your child will be able to become more comfortable in social situations, but everyone experiences some anxiety from time to time.

It is equally unhelpful to set too high a standard for your child's performance. A realistic goal does not demand that your child behave perfectly. Human beings are not perfect. Kids especially are not perfect. Sure, you want your child to do his or her best, but it's even more important that your child learns that it's okay to make mistakes, that we're all imperfect by nature.

What if you have more than one goal? It's quite likely that you'll want your child to work on more than one goal. Although it would be nice if your child could achieve all his goals simultaneously, it usually doesn't work this way. Typically, it makes more sense to work on certain goals first and others later on. Working on more than one goal at once can dilute your efforts, making it more difficult to see progress. In contrast, when you and your child work on one goal at a time, you can focus all your energy on that area. Your child will probably be surprised that by achieving one goal, the other goals will be much easier to accomplish later on.

How do you decide where to begin? In general, we believe the best approach is to work on the easiest goal first, thus boosting the child's confidence and giving her the sense that, "Hey, I can do this!" Sometimes, however, you don't have a lot of latitude in choosing your goals. If your child is missing school and experiencing falling grades because of social anxiety, you obviously need to address this before you work on handling anxiety in extracurricular activities.

Ultimately, the priority you and your child give to each of the goals you've written down is up to you. Keep in mind that there's really no right or wrong order. If your child starts working on one goal and you later realize that it would be better to work on a different goal, you can easily make the switch. The purpose of establishing priorities for the goals is to have a game plan, but game plans can always change. We suggest that you work through the steps in this book using one goal and switching to another goal only if necessary. Then you can go back and help your child work on achieving the other goals as well.

DEFINE YOUR OBJECTIVES

AFTER YOU AND your child have set the goal you want to work toward, the next step is to define your objectives. Sometimes in everyday speech the words "goal" and "objective" are used interchangeably, but we give them two distinct meanings in this context. Setting your goal answers the question, "What do I want my child to accomplish?" Defining your objective answers the question, "How will I know when my child has accomplished the goal?" or, "What will be different when my child reaches the goal?" Objectives are important because they are the signals that tell you and your child when he or she has been successful.

Typically, objectives involve changes in specific behaviors, thoughts, and feelings that occur when your child accomplishes the goal. For example, if you and your child have established a goal of his being more comfortable at family gatherings, objectives might include not throwing a tantrum before going to such functions, making eye contact and saying hello to family members, and sitting at the dinner table with the rest of the group. As you can see, when your child has reached his objectives, he has achieved his goal.

Let's look at another example of developing objectives for a specific goal.

Goal: My child will be more comfortable at school.

Objectives:
- My child will eat at least 50% of her food at lunch.
- My child will be able to use the restroom, rather than "holding it" all day.
- My child will make eye contact with the teacher and speak to her.
- My child will have at least one friend whom she can talk to during the day.
- My child will complain of fewer stomachaches in the morning.

You can see how objectives help define and personalize a goal. You can also see how objectives guide you, letting you know what kinds of things you'll need to do to help your child overcome social anxiety.

Now it's your turn. Decide which goal you and your child will work on first and develop specific objectives for that goal.

Goal: _____

(Look at your list of goals on page 70 and select one.)

Objectives:

- _____
- _____
- _____
- _____
- _____

If you're still not clear about how to set goals and define objectives, don't give up. It can seem like a simple task on the surface, but when you actually sit down and try to write things out, you realize it's more complex than it appears. Let's go through another example to see how the process works.

COREY'S EXAMPLE

COREY, A FIFTEEN-YEAR-OLD high school student with a strong fear of public speaking, had gone to great lengths to avoid participating in any activity that would require him to be in the spotlight, even for just a few minutes. His family was quite active in church, and several times he had been asked to do a reading. Despite it being awkward to say no, he always found a reason to decline. Similarly, although he was in the church youth group, and even was considered to be somewhat of a leader, he was unable to make announcements during the service about upcoming events.

His fear also affected him at school. Corey, typically an A student, received lower grades in classes that required public speaking. He always knew his material for any oral report he had to give, however, he was graded down for not making eye contact with the audience and talking too quickly. In addition, he never shared his opinion in class discussions, although he had plenty of ideas that he would have liked to share. His teachers knew he was bright and a good student, yet many commented that they "didn't really know him."

Corey's parents had always assumed their son was just shy, until they saw a television commercial about social anxiety disorder. After doing a little research on the Internet, his parents thought it would be worth having him evaluated by a psychologist. Corey had seemed to withdraw more and more with each year of school, and it really worried them.

Although Corey was initially reluctant to see a "shrink," he agreed that he wanted to overcome his fears. He felt angry that his anxiety was controlling him so much, and his anger served as a healthy source of motivation. After our initial sessions of gathering background information, determining the extent of the problem, and doing some education about the nature and treatment of social anxiety disorder, we were ready to set some goals.

Initially, this was Corey's goal:

My Goal: I want to be a great public speaker and never feel nervous again.

What do you think about the goal Corey set for himself? Can you see how the wording could be improved? Corey's goal was unrealistic. Even polished performers feel nervous sometimes. In fact, many of them believe if they don't experience some anxiety ahead of time, they won't have the needed energy to make it a good performance. They learn to manage their anxiety and channel it into enthusiasm.

In addition, Corey was expecting a lot of himself, wanting to be a "great" public speaker. It is difficult to define "great"—how would he know when he reached his goal? That's putting a lot of pressure on himself.

Corey was only fifteen, so this was a good first attempt at writing a goal. I just needed to help him revise it a bit, to make it more achievable.

Here is Corey's revised goal and the objectives we set for him.

Goal: I want to become more comfortable with public speaking.

Objectives:
- I will accept invitations to do readings at church.
- I will make announcements for the church youth group during the service.
- I will ask questions and express my opinion during classes.
- I will make eye contact and talk more slowly during oral presentations.

Do you see how Corey's goal is more manageable now? No longer does he have to be a "great" public speaker in order to succeed. He can also forgive himself a small amount of nervousness. His objectives are realistic and attainable, and they allow him to recognize when he has achieved his goal.

Keep in mind that we're not saying that meeting these objectives will be easy. It will take a lot of hard work and a good dose of patience on Corey's part. Writing out his goal and objectives is a great start, though. He's got an all-important game plan, and of course his parents will be there to help him follow the plan.

A TOUGH JOB

WE KNOW WE'RE asking you to wear many different hats. Not only do you have to be the parent, but you also need to be the coach, not to mention the cheerleader—rooting for your child even when the game is rough. Remember that as therapists, we're usually working with the parents and their child, guiding them in this process. Many of you will make good progress on your own, but if you run into problems, it's not a sign of failure to seek help. Whether you go through this book on your own or as an adjunct to therapy, we know you can do it! We'll be right here cheering for both you and your child.

|||||||||||||||||||||||||||||||||||||||||||||||||||||||||||||||||||||||||||||||

CHAPTER 5

Easing Through the Fear

Relaxation Exercises for Kids

PATTY CALLED me prior to our first appointment to fill me in on her daughter's difficulties before we met. Samantha, who was eight years old, suffered from frequent headaches and stomachaches. Her pediatrician referred them to me after running some tests and finding no medical cause for her symptoms. The doctor suspected that anxiety was the primary culprit in causing her pain. Samantha's parents were afraid she wouldn't participate in treatment, though. She had thus far resisted all attempts to label her difficulties as being related to anxiety.

Patty told me that Samantha was having some social difficulties at school. She was shy and quiet but had one good friend who had always been in her classes. This year, however, the girls had been assigned to different teachers. Samantha had difficulty making new friends in her class and cried after school each day, saying that no one liked her. Then, to make matters worse, a few weeks into the school year Samantha's teacher developed problems with her pregnancy and had to go on bed rest. Samantha didn't seem to click with the substitute teacher and began complaining of headaches and stomachaches.

Patty, her husband, and the doctor had all talked to Samantha about the possibility that her stomachaches and headaches were caused by her "worrying" too much. Samantha didn't want to talk about the issues at school, however. Rather, she insisted that she was sick and needed to stay home.

The background information Patty provided me was useful and gave me a heads-up on how I needed to approach Samantha. I planned to explain to Samantha that her pain was real—her head and stomach truly did hurt at times. I wouldn't push too hard in the beginning on making the connection between her headaches and stomachaches and her anxiety at school. I'd explain to her that we were going to work on making her feel better—making those headaches and stomachaches go away. She was willing to work on that.

I discussed with Samantha and her parents how I would teach them relaxation techniques that would help Samantha's stomachaches and headaches get better. Later, we'd address how her stomachaches and headaches were related to her anxiety. But for now, we'd focus on the skills to help Samantha feel more comfortable and in control. The rest of this chapter will give you the same information that I gave to Samantha's parents—what you need to know to help your child learn to relax. The first step in this process is teaching your child how to rate his or her anxiety level.

RATING ANXIETY LEVELS

ANXIETY-PRONE CHILDREN are often not adept at discerning different levels of fear and discomfort. They're likely to view situations in an all-or-nothing fashion. For example, they may say to themselves, "I'm freaking out!" at the slightest provocation. An important task, then, is to teach your child that there are many different levels of fear and anxiety and it's helpful to be able to rate these levels in a meaningful way.

When we work with adults, we have them rate their anxiety on a 0 to 10 scale. A 10 is the most anxious or afraid they've ever been in their entire life. A 0, on the other hand, is the most relaxed they've ever been. These numbers are the person's own personal interpretation of his or her anxiety level. An anxiety level of 5 may be very different for one person than for another. The scale works equally well for adolescents.

ANXIETY RATING SCALE

NONE	1
Relaxed, no	
discomfort	2
MILD	3
Not quite relaxed,	
just noticable discomfort	4
MODERATE	5
Definite discomfort	
but managing it	6
SEVERE	7
Extremely uncomfortable,	
feel it becoming unmanageable	8
VERY SEVERE	9
Worst I have ever felt—	
overwhelming	10

For younger children, we more often use the concept of a fear thermometer. You can draw your own if you're artistically inclined; the one we like the best is from Aureen Pinto Wagner's *Up and Down the Worry Hill*. She's graciously given us permission to include it for your use.

Explain the idea of rating anxiety levels to your child. Some children relate more to the word "worry" than fear or anxiety. If this is the case, call it the worry thermometer or the worry scale. In Samantha's case, she was so focused on her physical symptoms that her parents had her rate her physical discomfort at first. Simply make adjustments to the scale using whatever terminology is appropriate to your child's situation.

Have your child practice rating his anxiety level throughout the day and in many different circumstances. For example, before eating breakfast on a typical school day, show your child the fear thermometer and have him rate how he's feeling. Do this many times at periodic intervals until your child becomes comfortable with the process. It can help to keep a log of the ratings so you can see any particular patterns that emerge. Here's a brief example of how this might look.

The _____ Thermometer

10. Out of Control! Ballistic!
9. Can't Handle It.
8. Really Tough.
7. Pretty Tough.
6. Getting Tough.
5. Not too Good.
4. Starting to Bother.
3. Just a Little Uneasy.
2. A Little Twinge.
1. Piece of Cake!

From Aureen P. Wagner, Ph.D., *Worried No More*. Copyright © 2001. Used with permission.

FEAR RATING LOG

DATE/TIME	SITUATION	FEAR RATING
Friday, 7:30 a.m.	Getting ready for school	6
Friday, 3:30 p.m.	Home from school	0
Friday, 6:30 p.m.	Going out, kids staying with sitter	4

Now that your child has mastered rating personal anxiety levels, the next step is to learn a simple yet highly effective breathing technique that can significantly reduce anxious symptoms and reactions. We first explain the importance of this type of breathing and then show you how to teach it to your child.

THE HIDDEN POWER OF BREATHING

INTELLECTUALLY, WE KNOW that breathing is fundamental to life, but we usually take this amazing process for granted. We don't pay attention to how we breathe, and for many people prone to anxiety, breathing patterns become problematic.

Imagine your child entering a room full of other kids she doesn't know. She's worried what they will think about her. What happens to her breathing? Most likely, it becomes rapid and shallow. She may even feel short of breath, as if she's gasping for air.

Recall from Chapter 2 how human beings are biologically programmed to respond with "fight or flight" when confronted with a dangerous situation. This rapid and shallow breathing actually leads to complex physiological reactions that prepare one's body to respond quickly to an emergency. This system worked exceedingly well in previous eras when threats to survival were often physical,

such as fighting off an enemy while hunting for food. But when your child is afraid to enter a roomful of people because of a fear of scrutiny or disapproval, there's no need for these physical changes. Your child's breathing is in excess of her metabolic needs. This is called overbreathing or, in its extreme form, hyperventilation.

Overbreathing and hyperventilation can produce a number of physical symptoms: light-headedness, dizziness, shortness of breath, heart palpitations, tingling sensations, chest pain, tremors, sweating, dry mouth, difficulty swallowing, and weakness. Does this list sound familiar?

When your child or adolescent experiences many of these physical symptoms at once, she's probably in an acute state of hyperventilation. In fact, 60 percent of all panic attacks are accompanied by acute hyperventilation. But your child doesn't have to be huffing and puffing or gasping for air to be hyperventilating. Even slight alterations in breathing patterns can produce physiologic changes in one's body chemistry, thus leading to some of symptoms listed above.

Here are some signs indicating your child may be chroni overbreathing:

- frequent yawning or sighing
- sounding breathless when speaking
- breathing from the upper chest
- breathing rapidly

Fortunately, with training and practice, almost anyone ca exert conscious control over his or her breathing patterns. turn can help manage anxiety. The breathing technique has many names: diaphragmatic breathing, abdomina breathing, controlled breathing, or paced breathing. I the name, this slow and deep manner of breathing is a ural relaxant—one that can be used to alleviate anxi of social situations.

What is diaphragmatic breathing? Have you ever noticed how a baby breathes? His or her belly rises and falls rhythmically with each breath? We're born knowing how to breathe the "correct" way, and we still breathe this way when we sleep. But stress, anxiety, and bad habits can prevent people from routinely doing what once came naturally.

The diaphragm is a large umbrella-shaped muscle that separates the chest cavity from the abdominal cavity. It is intimately involved in the process of inhaling and exhaling air. As you inhale, the diaphragm descends to allow room for the increased air volume. Then as you exhale, the diaphragm rises upward as air is released from the lungs.

Let's look at what happens if your muscles are tense, as they might be when you're anxious. If your stomach muscles are tense when the diaphragm descends to accommodate the air being inhaled, the diaphragm meets with resistance. It cannot move as far down as it ordinarily would. There isn't as much room for air to flow in, and so your breathing is shallow. Poor posture can also prevent the diaphragm from moving freely as it needs to.

Before you get started teaching your child this breathing technique, there are three points you need to remember about diaphragmatic breathing:

1. Have your child inhale and exhale through the nose. Breathing through the mouth increases the possibility of hyperventilating.
2. As your child inhales, the abdomen should extend outward. You can think of this as making room for the air that's being taken in. As your child exhales, the abdomen flattens as the air is pushed out. This may be exactly the opposite of how your child normally breathes, especially when anxious.
3. Help your child concentrate on breathing slowly and deeply.

Although this may not be the way you or your child is accustomed to breathing and may feel awkward at first, this is the way our bodies were designed. It's truly a healthier way to breathe.

Teaching your child diaphragmatic breathing. We take you step-by-step through the process of teaching your child to breathe this way. You may want to spend some time learning and practicing this method of breathing yourself before you teach it to your child.

Let's look at how Patty taught Samantha diaphragmatic breathing. The easiest way to begin is to have your child lie on the floor and place a light tissue box on his or her abdomen, directly above the navel. Samantha wanted to put a small stuffed animal on her belly instead, which works just as well. Patty told Samantha to take slow breaths as she watched Mr. Bear rise as she breathed in—to make room for the air—and fall as she breathed out. Patty also had Samantha imagine a balloon in her belly, getting bigger and then smaller with each breath. She reminded Samantha to breathe through her nose. They practiced this twice a day, five minutes each time. Samantha enjoyed and looked forward to these practice sessions.

After they practiced this for several days, they did the same procedure but without Mr. Bear. Instead, Patty had her daughter place one hand on her belly, with her little finger resting just above her belly button. She told Samantha to feel her hand rise and fall as she inhaled and exhaled (breathed in and out). They practiced this way for another few days until Samantha felt comfortable. Then they did the same thing but with Samantha's hands at her sides.

Next, they continued the breathing practice, but Patty had Samantha vary her body position. For example, Samantha practiced diaphragmatic breathing while lying on her side. Then she tried it sitting up. Finally, Samantha learned to breathe this way while standing. This took several weeks of practice for Samantha to become proficient at breathing diaphragmatically in a variety of positions.

Using diaphragmatic breathing. Your and your child's diligent practice is soon going to pay off. Your child is ready to branch out and apply this way of breathing throughout his or her daily activities. Here's see how this worked for Samantha.

First, Patty began having Samantha "check in" with her breathing frequently throughout the day. When Samantha was home, they had a nonverbal cue that signaled Samantha briefly to stop what she was doing and notice her breathing. Was she breathing slowly and deeply? Or was she breathing rapidly and from the chest? They also worked out some set times at school (when the bell rang between classes, for example) when Samantha was to do a quick breathing check. Patty worked with Samantha to notice how her breathing changed depending on what was going on around her.

As Samantha enjoyed some success with the breathing technique, she became more open to talking about the things bothering her at school. She even conceded that maybe her being "worked up" so much of the time was leading her to experience the headaches and stomachaches. This was a major breakthrough and allowed Patty to go a step farther in teaching the breathing technique.

Patty coached Samantha to use this "belly breathing" when she was in an anxiety-arousing situation. She told Samantha to try to catch her fear level in the early stages; she'd have a much better chance for success. In other words, Samantha shouldn't wait until she was at level 8 on her fear thermometer and then try breathing techniques to stop the scary feelings. It wouldn't work nearly as well as taking a few moments to concentrate on breathing slowly and deeply when her fear was at level 3.

Samantha gradually began trying the diaphragmatic breathing during stressful times at school. Patty usually had to prompt her ahead of time. The night before they would go over situations that might be problematic. For example, Samantha had difficulty when it was time to go to PE. This class always made her nervous because she perceived the PE teacher as being "strict" and "mean." Patty encouraged Samantha to check in with her breathing, rate her fear level, and do some deep breathing ten minutes before it was time to go to PE. This gave Samantha a sense of control, and she reported that her stomach and head hurt less, as well.

Of course, the diaphragmatic breathing didn't totally take away Samantha's anxiety. This is simply one tool. But she'd learned the basics of a coping skill she could continue practicing and using while working on other ways to decrease her fears.

APPLIED RELAXATION TRAINING

APPLIED RELAXATION TRAINING combines several well-known and proven relaxation techniques in a way that allows you to relax rapidly even in anxious situations. It takes times and practice to reach the point of being able to relax on command, but it can be done.

Applied relaxation training was developed in the late 1980s by the Swedish physician Lars-Goran Öst, who is well-known for his work in anxiety disorders. Öst wanted to find a way to help his phobic patients more easily enter their feared situations. To do this, he creatively combined several relaxation techniques that armed his patients with exactly what they needed—a powerful, fast, and reliable method to relieve their anxiety. By employing these relaxation techniques, even severely phobic patients were able to manage their anxiety while facing their fears.

Applied relaxation training involves six stages, and each stage builds on the previous one. This isn't a quick fix, so you'll have to encourage your child to be patient. Devote about twenty minutes a day to practice, and give your child one or two weeks to become comfortable with each stage. Keep in mind that the earlier stages will take more time to master than the later ones. As your child becomes more adept at these relaxation techniques, it will take less practice time and become more a matter of refining and applying the skills.

Stage 1: Progressive muscle relaxation (PMR). The goal of this first stage is to help your child recognize the difference between how his muscles feel when they're tense and how they feel when they're relaxed. You might think you automatically know this, but many people—children included—experience chronic muscle tension without even realizing it. By practicing PMR, your child will quickly begin to scan the body for muscle tension and be able to relax any trouble spots on command.

To teach your child PMR, you may find it helpful to tape-record the instructions below and go through them yourself a few times first. After that, you'll probably be familiar enough with the procedure that you won't need the tape. Or simply follow the script we've included on pages 94–95. For younger children, we've included an alternative script that is a bit more kid-friendly, on pages 96–100.

These are the basic instructions:

1. Find a comfortable, quiet place to sit or lie down.
2. Take a deep breath from your diaphragm (belly).
3. Tense each muscle group one at a time following the list below. Notice what the tension feels like. Hold the tension for five to ten seconds.
4. Release the tension. Focus on how relaxed the muscle feels.
5. Take another deep breath.
6. Repeat procedure with each muscle group.

Below are the major muscle groups. Tense and release each one in order.

Your head

- Clench your teeth and pull the corners of your mouth back in a forced smile.
- Close your eyes tightly.
- Open your eyes as wide as you can.

Your neck and shoulders

- Press your head to your right shoulder, then your left.
- Press your chin toward your chest.
- Tilt your head toward your back. Don't force it too far, though.
- Raise your shoulders up toward your ears in a big shrug.

Your arms and hands

- Tighten your hands into fists.
- Tighten the muscles in your upper body by making a fist and bending your arms up at the elbows.
- Press your hand firmly into the surface where you're practicing.

Your chest

- Take a deep breath and puff out your chest.
- Tighten your chest muscles.

Your back

- Arch your back.

Your abdomen

- Push your abdomen out as far as you can.
- Pull your abdomen in tight toward your spine.

Your hips, legs, and feet

- Tighten your buttocks.
- Push the soles of your feet down into the floor. If you're lying down, press your heels.
- Flex your toes upward.

Practice with your child this way at least once a day. It should take approximately fifteen to twenty minutes to go through the entire process. Remember, the goal at this stage is to really notice the difference between tension and relaxation.

Stage 2: Release-only relaxation. In this stage you omit the first part of PMR, the tensing part, and instead focus only on relaxing each of the muscle groups in turn. This will shorten the time the process takes and allow your child to reach a state of deep relaxation more quickly.

Have your child begin in a comfortable position, either sitting or lying down. Have your child focus on his breathing for a few minutes. Have him concentrate on taking deep belly breaths. Now progress through the muscle groups and gently give the suggestion to relax each muscle and allow the tension to slip effortlessly away. You can intensify the relaxation experience by having your child imagine the muscle being heavy and warm. After you've progressed through the entire body, encourage your child to spend a few minutes breathing deeply. Have him scan his body for any remaining tension. Focus on any muscles that are still tense and spend a moment relaxing those areas.

Don't rush through this stage. It may seem easier than progressive muscle relaxation, but it's actually more difficult because your child is relaxing the muscles entirely through the power of the mind.

Stage 3: Cue-controlled relaxation. This is a simple idea that involves pairing a word with a relaxed physical state. With enough repetition of this pairing, the body learns to associate the relaxed condition with the word. With enough time spent conditioning the body and mind in this way, your child will use the word to direct her body to calm down, even in anxiety-arousing situations.

Your child can select any word or short phrase to be the cue. Many people use a single word, such as "relax" or "calm," but you could just as easily use a phrase. You also can have your child use a physical gesture as the cue—either alone or in combination with a word or phrase—such as touching a hand to the side of the body. The details don't matter much; what counts is whether the cue works for your child.

Here are the instructions to give your child:

1. Take a few deep breaths. As you do, imagine all your worries floating away.

2. Using release-only relaxation, spend a few minutes scanning your body for tension, letting all of it slip away.

3. Once you're relaxed, silently say your cue word every time you exhale.

4. Continue inhaling deeply through your nose, holding the breath for a few seconds, and then exhaling while silently saying your cue word or phrase. Spend a few minutes on this step.

With practice, your child should be able to relax completely in about two or three minutes. Again, it may take several weeks of practice to get to this point. In the beginning, have your child do as many brief mini-relaxation sessions as possible using the cue. This will enhance the conditioning process. In other words, the frequent pairing of a relaxed state with the cue will give your child the power to use the cue later, when he or she is anxious.

Stage 4: Differential relaxation. The purpose of this stage is to have your child become accustomed to relaxing the body in different positions and situations, not just while lying down or sitting comfortably in a quiet room. Remember, the purpose of applied relaxation is eventually to be able to relax quickly while in a stressful situation.

If your child has been practicing the relaxation exercises while lying down, now have her do them in a comfortable chair. Next, move on to a harder, straight-backed chair. We're mainly talking about practicing the cue-controlled relaxation, but it may also be helpful to review progressive muscle and release-only relaxation in different contexts as well.

Try adding distractions when your child practices relaxing. Have the radio or the TV on in the background. Have your child practice in a different room. Practice standing up. The idea is gradually to add more "real-life" aspects into the practice sessions.

Stage 5: Rapid relaxation. As the name implies, the goal of this stage is to have your child shorten the time needed to relax down to about thirty seconds and to do so frequently throughout the day.

Recall how in cue-controlled relaxation, your child picked a word to say while breathing deeply and scanning for tension. In this stage, your child picks another kind of cue—a reminder to relax throughout the day. For example, your child might select her watch as a reminder. You can even put a piece of colored tape on it or tie a string around the band to remind her in the beginning. Every time she looks at her watch during the day, it should remind her to

- take a deep breath
- say the cue word
- scan her body for tension
- release the tightness from these muscles

The idea of this stage is to have some kind of reminder to relax that your child will notice frequently throughout the day.

Stage 6: Applied relaxation. Your child is now ready to begin applying these relaxation skills when in anxiety-producing situations. Remember, this technique will probably not take away your child's anxiety completely. It will, however, be a powerful tool to help your child manage his anxiety.

As we noted earlier in the chapter, one of the keys to explain to your child is to catch anxiety early, when it's at a mild level. Your child will learn that he can function in spite of anxiety, especially when the anxiety isn't overwhelming yet. If your child waits until he's in a state of panic, it is much harder, if not impossible, to bring his anxiety under control using relaxation techniques alone. This is one reason why practicing the previous stages is so crucial. By doing so, your child gains plenty of experience in regularly scanning his body for tension and recognizing what areas of his body tend to tense up first.

As soon as your child notices any signs of tension or anxiety, have her begin these steps:

1. Take two or three deep breaths, using your diaphragmatic breathing skills.
2. Think your cue word to yourself as you continue to breathe slowly and deeply.
3. Scan your body for tension and focus on relaxing those muscles that feel tense.

Remind your child to be patient; as we've said, this takes a lot of practice. And remember, if your child brings his anxiety down even a notch or two, it makes a big difference in how he feels.

IMAGERY TRAINING

ANOTHER TYPE OF relaxation exercise you can teach your child involves the use of imagery. While not a substitute for learning diaphragmatic breathing or applied relaxation training, imagery training can be a useful addition to your child's repertoire of anxiety management strategies. Children often have vivid imaginations and readily learn this relaxation technique. It differs from the other methods we've described primarily in that your child focuses on a scene rather than on his or her body.

Here's a sample miniscript for an imagery relaxation exercise:

Begin by taking a few deep breaths. Now imagine that you are outside on a pleasantly warm summer day. You are resting on a large blanket next to a beautiful small lake. You can feel the warmth of the sun as it shines down on you. The warm sunshine helps you feel relaxed. You can feel the warmth of the sun on your skin and in your muscles.

Each time you breathe in, you feel the fresh, clean air enter your lungs, and you feel refreshed. Each time you breathe out, you feel relaxed, comfortable, and content.

You can hear the soft sound of the wind as it blows gently through the leaves of the nearby trees. Focus on this sound as you hear the breeze each time it begins and notice when it ends.

As you look up into the bright blue sky, you see a few puffy, white clouds. You notice how they move ever so slightly, being carried only by the gentle breeze. Imagine what it must feel like to be able to float so easily, to feel so light.

As you continue to relax, you look at the water. You see a few small water bugs skimming along the top of the water. They look like they are playing. You continue to watch them until a leaf falls and lands on the surface of the water. When the leaf hits the water, you see ripples spreading out into circles.

Continue to allow yourself to relax, just focusing on whatever parts of this scene are most pleasant.

This is just one example of what you can do with imagery. Common examples that people select for relaxation imagery involve scenes in the woods, lying on a raft in a swimming pool, taking a nap in a hammock, relaxing in a meadow, sitting by the ocean, and so on. The best scenes to use are ones your child can imagine vividly. Have your child concentrate on all the details and use all of his senses to complete the picture.

A QUICK REVIEW: WHY LEARNING TO RELAX IS SO IMPORTANT

WE HOPE YOUR child has enjoyed some success with learning to relax and it's obvious to you why these skills are important to develop. By way of summary, however, we review some of the reasons below:

- Just like Samantha with her stomachaches and headaches, many children with anxiety problems suffer from a number of related physical symptoms. Learning relaxation exercises makes sense to these kids. They're often focused on the physical sensations, and this is one way to target these problems directly.

- A relaxed physical body is less prone to experiencing worrisome thoughts. It's as if those "fear pathways" in the brain aren't dug as deep when the body is at ease.
- Knowing how to relax—especially if your child gets to the point where he or she can relax fairly quickly—will help your child with the work in the chapters to come, particularly in entering feared situations during "exposure therapy."

If you've thus far read through only this chapter, now is the time to go back, dig in, and work with your child on learning these relaxation techniques. It can seem like a lot of effort, but it's well worth it. If you've already progressed through this chapter and your child has to some degree mastered these skills, you're ready to move ahead to the next chapter, "Thinking It Through."

PROGRESSIVE MUSCLE RELAXATION SCRIPT

LET'S BEGIN BY taking in a deep breath, holding it in for a second or two, and letting it go whenever you feel ready . . . Now let's do the same thing again . . . Take a deep breath, hold it in for a second or two, then let it go. Notice how relaxed your body begins to feel . . . Let your breathing return to normal, whatever is normal for you. If your breathing is fast, let it be fast . . . if it is slow, let it be slow.

Now take your hands and tighten them into fists . . . Hold them tight and notice how it feels . . . Notice the tension in your hands, wrists, and forearms . . . focus on it . . . and notice the change as you let the tension go, letting your hands relax . . .

Tighten the muscles in your upper arms, like you are "making a muscle" with each arm or you are lifting something very heavy. Notice how strong the muscles in your upper arms feel . . . notice the tightness, the tension. Now let your arms relax and notice how the relaxation feels, how it feels different from the tension. Focus on the feeling of relaxation . . .

Now bring your shoulders up toward your ears and tighten the muscles in your shoulders. Again, focus on the tightness in those muscles . . . and notice the change as you let your shoulders relax . . . As your shoulders relax even more, they may feel just a little bit heavy as they continue to relax . . .

Now we are going to work on relaxing some of the muscles around your head . . . Clench your teeth a bit—not too hard, but enough so you can feel some tension in your jaws, your cheeks, and your neck . . . Again, focus on the tension and notice the change when you let the tension go . . . letting those muscles relax . . .

Close your eyes tightly so you can feel the tension in the muscles and skin all around your eyes . . . Focus on it . . . and let it go . . .

Open your eyes as wide as you can . . . You will notice some tension in your forehead, maybe a little bit in the muscles on the side of the head . . . Let it relax, let it go . . .

Now take a deep breath and puff out your chest . . . Hold the air in and notice how your chest feels . . . Pay attention to the feeling there as you let the air out slowly . . .

Tighten the muscles in your chest and upper back . . . Hold the tension . . . and now let it go . . . Notice how much easier it is to breathe . . . Maybe you feel like taking in a deep breath and letting it out slowly . . .

Now tighten the muscles in your stomach . . . Notice how the tension feels . . . then let it go . . . Once again, you may feel like taking in a deep breath and letting the air out slowly . . . Your breathing gets easier as these muscles relax . . .

Now, tighten the muscles in your seat, your rear end . . . You may feel like they are pushing you up in your chair . . . Focus on the tension—these muscles are very strong . . . Now focus on the feeling as you let them relax . . . and unwind . . .

Moving down to your legs, tighten the muscles in your upper legs . . . Notice how strong these muscles feel . . . then let them relax . . .

Now curl your toes upward, try to point them toward the ceiling . . . Notice the tension in your feet and lower legs . . . Focus on it . . . and let it go, let your feet and legs relax . . .

Take a few moments to notice how relaxed your body can feel . . . Remember what this relaxation feels like . . . With practice, you will be able to relax more completely, and in any situation . . . Take your time . . . You can open your eyes whenever you want . . .

RELAXATION TRAINING SCRIPT
FOR YOUNG CHILDREN

Introduction

Today we're going to do some special kinds of exercises called *relaxation exercises*. These exercises help you learn how to relax when you're feeling uptight and help you get rid of those butterflies-in-your-stomach kinds of feelings. They're also kind of neat, because you can do some of them without anybody noticing.

To get the best feelings from these exercises, there are some rules you must follow. First, you must do exactly what I say, even if it seems kind of silly. Second, you must try hard to do what I say. Third, you must pay attention to your body. In these exercises, pay attention to how your muscles feel when they are tight and when they are loose and relaxed. And fourth, you must practice. The more you practice, the more relaxed you can get.

Are you ready to begin? Okay. First, get as comfortable as you can in your chair. Sit back, get both feet on the floor, and just let your arms hang loose. That's fine. Now close your eyes and don't open them until I say to. Remember to follow my instructions very carefully, try hard, and pay attention to your body. Here we go.

Hands and Arms

Pretend you have a whole lemon in your left hand. Now squeeze it hard. Try to squeeze all the juice out. Feel the tightness in your hand and arm as you squeeze. Now drop the lemon. Notice how your muscles feel when they are relaxed. Take another lemon and squeeze it. Try to squeeze this one harder than you did the first one. That's right. Real hard. Now drop your lemon and relax. See how much better your hand and arm feel when they are relaxed. Once again, take a lemon in your left hand and squeeze all the juice out. Don't leave a single drop. Squeeze hard. Good. Now relax and let the lemon fall from your hand. (Repeat the process for the right hand and arm.)

Arms and Shoulders

Pretend you are a furry, lazy cat. You want to stretch. Stretch your arms out in front of you. Raise them up high over your head. Way back. Feel the pull in your shoulders. Stretch higher. Now just let your arms drop back to your side. Okay, kitten, let's stretch again. Stretch your arms out in front of you. Raise them over your head. Pull them back, way back. Pull hard. Now let them drop quickly. Good. Notice how your shoulders feel more relaxed. This time let's have a great big stretch. Try to touch the ceiling. Stretch your arms way out in front of you. Raise them way up high over your head. Push them way, way back. Feel the tension and pull in your arms and shoulders. Hold tight, now. Great. Let them drop very quickly and feel how good it is to be relaxed. It feels good and warm and lazy.

Shoulders and Neck

Now pretend you are a turtle. You're sitting out on a rock by a nice peaceful pond, just relaxing in the warm sun. It feels nice and warm and safe here. Uh-oh! You sense danger. Pull your head into your house. Try to pull your shoulders up to your ears and push your head down into your shoulders. Hold it tight. It isn't easy to be a turtle in a shell. The danger is past now. You can come out into the warm sunshine, and once again, you can relax and feel the warm sunshine. Watch out now! More danger. Hurry, pull your head back into your house and hold it tight. You have to be closed in tight to protect yourself. Okay, you can relax now. Bring your head out and let your shoulders relax. It feels much better to be relaxed than to be all tight. One more time, now. Danger! Pull your head in. Push your shoulders way up to your ears and hold tight. Don't let even a tiny piece of your head show outside your shell. Hold it. Feel the tenseness in your neck and shoulders. Okay. You can come out now. It's safe again. Relax and feel comfortable in your safety. There's no more danger. Nothing to worry about. Nothing to be afraid of. You feel good.

Jaw

You have a giant jawbreaker bubble gum in your mouth. It's very hard to chew. Bite down on it. Hard! Let your neck muscles help you. Now relax. Just let your jaw hang loose. It feels good just to let your jaw drop. Okay, let's tackle that jawbreaker again now. Bite down. Hard! Try to squeeze it out between your teeth. That's good. You're really tearing that gum up. Now relax again. Just let your jaw drop off your face. It feels so good just to let go and not have to fight that bubble gum. Okay, one more time. We're really going to tear it up this time. Bite down. Hard as you can. Harder. Oh, you're really working hard. Good. Now relax. Try to relax your whole body. You've beaten the bubble gum. Let yourself go as loose as you can.

Face and Nose

Here comes a pesky old fly. He has landed on your nose. Try to get him off without using your hands. That's right, wrinkle up your nose. Make as many wrinkles in your nose as you can. Scrunch your nose up real hard. Good. You've chased him away. Now you can re-lax your nose. Oops, here he comes back again. Right back in the middle of your nose. Wrinkle up your nose again. Shoo him off. Wrinkle it up hard. Hold it just as tight as you can. Okay, he flew away. You can relax your face. When you scrunch up your nose, your cheeks and your mouth and your forehead and your eyes all help you, and they get tight, too. So when you relax your nose, your whole face relaxes, too, and that feels good. Uh-oh. That old fly has come back, but this time he's on your forehead. Make lots of wrin-kles. Try to catch him between all those wrinkles. Hold it tight, now. Okay, you can let go. He's gone for good. Now you can just relax. Let your face go smooth, no wrinkles anywhere. Your face feels nice and smooth and relaxed.

Stomach

Hey! Here comes a cute baby elephant. But he's not watching where he's going. He doesn't see you lying there in the grass, and he's about to step on your stomach. Don't move. You don't have time to get out of the way. Just get ready for him. Make your stomach very hard. Tighten up your stomach muscles real tight. Hold it. It looks like he is going the other way. You can relax now. Let your stomach go soft. Let it be as relaxed as you can. That feels so much better. Oops, he's coming this way again. Get ready. Tighten up your stomach. Real hard. If he steps on you when your stomach is hard, it won't hurt. Make your stomach into a rock. Okay, he's moving away again. You can relax now. Kind of settle down, get comfortable, and relax. Feel the difference between a tight stomach and a relaxed one. That's how we want it to feel—nice and loose and relaxed. You won't believe this, but this time he's really coming your way and not turning around. He's headed straight for you. Tighten up. Tighten hard. Here he comes. This is really it. You've got to hold on tight. He's stepping on you. He's stepped over you. Now he's gone for good. You can relax completely. You're safe. Everything is okay, and you feel nice and relaxed.

This time imagine that you want to squeeze through a narrow fence, and the boards have splinters on them. You'll have to make yourself very skinny if you're going to make it through. Suck your stomach in. Try to squeeze it up against your backbone. Try to be as skinny as you can. You've got to get through. Now relax. You don't have to be skinny now. Just relax and feel your stomach being warm and loose. Okay, let's try to get through that fence now. Squeeze up your stomach. Get it real small and tight. Get as skinny as you can. Hold tight, now. You can squeeze through. You can get through that skinny little fence and no splinters. You can relax now. Settle back and let your stomach come back out where it belongs. You can feel really good now. You've done fine.

Legs and Feet

Now pretend that you are standing barefoot in a big, fat mud puddle. Squish your toes down deep in the mud. Try to get your feet down to the bottom of the mud puddle. You'll probably need your legs to help you push. Push down, spread your toes apart, and feel the mud squish up between your toes. Now step out of the mud puddle. Relax your feet. Let your toes go loose and feel how nice that is. It feels good to be relaxed. Back into the mud puddle. Squish your toes down. Let your leg muscles help you push your feet down. Push your feet. Hard. Try to squeeze that mud puddle dry. Okay. Come back out now. Relax your feet, relax your legs, relax your toes. It feels so good to be relaxed. No tenseness anywhere. Your feel kind of warm and tingly.

Conclusion

Stay as relaxed as you can. Let your whole body go limp and feel all your muscles relaxed. In a few minutes I will ask you to open your eyes, and that will be the end of this session. As you go through the day, remember how good it feels to be relaxed. Sometimes you have to make yourself tighter before you can be relaxed, just as we did in these exercises. Practice these exercises every day to get more and more relaxed. A good time to practice is at night, after you have gone to bed and the lights are out and you won't be disturbed. It will help you get to sleep. Then, when you are a really good relaxer, you can help yourself relax at school. Just remember the elephant, or the jawbreaker, or the mud puddle, and you can do our exercises and nobody will know. Today is a good day. You've worked hard, and it feels good to work hard. Very slowly now, open your eyes and wiggle your muscles around a little. Very good. You've done a good job. You're going to be a super relaxer.

|||||||||||||||||||||||||||||||||||||||||||||||||||||||||||||||||||||||||||||

CHAPTER 6

Thinking It Through

*Cognitive Therapy Techniques
You Can Teach Your Child*

NOW THAT you've taught your child some relaxation techniques—ways to help handle the body's reaction to fear—we're going to show you how to help your child manage some of the mental reactions to fear and anxiety. Mental reactions are those thoughts and worries that pop into your child's mind, often generating significant stress and periods of "emotional meltdown." The strategies we introduce are part of what's called cognitive therapy.

In the last few decades, mental health professionals have become very aware of the strong influence our thoughts exert on our emotions and behavior. The psychologist Albert Ellis was one of the first to devise therapeutic techniques aimed at changing irrational cognitions, or thoughts that lead to unnecessary distress. His work in 1970 was followed by further theory and clinical strategies supported by a strong body of research. Contributions from the psychologists Michael Mahoney in 1971 and Donald Michenbaum in 1974 helped to build an impressive array of evidence that modifying your thoughts can truly lead to positive changes in feelings and behavior. Other pioneers in cognitive therapy include the psychiatrists Aaron

Beck and David Burns. More recently, the psychologist Richard Heimburg has demonstrated that many of these ideas can be helpful in alleviating social anxiety disorder.

Children suffering from social anxiety can benefit greatly from learning cognitive therapy techniques, although because of their age and mental ability, some of the strategies must be adapted. In the sections that follow, we present the basic ideas you need to know and show you how to teach them to your child.

THE RELATIONSHIP AMONG THOUGHTS, FEELINGS, AND BEHAVIOR

THINK OF A recent time in your own life when you were upset or worried. What was the situation? Let's say your boss told you he wants to meet with you in the morning to discuss a few things. What thoughts came to mind? Perhaps you said to yourself, "Oh, boy. What have I done this time?" Or maybe you thought, "Oh, good. Maybe he's going to give me that raise we've been discussing."

How would you feel in each of these scenarios? Can you see that your feelings would depend on your thoughts? If you thought you were going to get criticized, you'd feel upset and perhaps angry. If you thought you were going to get a raise, you'd feel pleased and excited.

How would these thoughts and feelings affect your behavior? In the first case, you might spend the rest of the day avoiding your boss. In the latter case, you'd probably be energized, walking around with a bounce in your step.

Many people think that a specific event causes them to feel and act a certain way. Rather, as you can see from the above example, it's the *interpretation* of these events (what we tell ourselves about the event) that gives rise to our feelings and actions.

Below are a few examples to go through with your child that will help demonstrate the relationship among thoughts, feelings, and behavior. Read the following scenarios to (or with) your child and have him or her answer the subsequent questions. Discuss your child's responses, but keep a neutral attitude. There are no right or wrong answers, just possible different ways that someone might view an event.

The Girls by the Swings

Imagine that you're on the playground at recess. There are a group of girls talking by the swings. They are giggling, looking like they're having fun. You'd like to join them. You walk toward them and say hi. No one looks up or says anything to you.

What do you tell yourself about what happened? (Thoughts)
a) Those girls are such snobs.
b) I'm such a loser. No one wants to be my friend.
c) They must not have heard me.
d) Other possibilities?

How do you feel? (Feelings)
a) Angry
b) Sad
c) Not much of anything
d) Other possibilities

What do you do? (Behavior)
a) Stomp off
b) Walk off with head down
c) Move closer and say hi louder so they can hear me
d) Other possibilities?

Can your child begin to see how her thoughts affect her feelings, and subsequently, her behavior? Don't expect your child to understand this perfectly. This can be a difficult concept even for adults, so be patient with your child as she's trying to get the hang of it. Also be sure to praise your child's efforts at simply paying attention to the scenario and going through the exercise with you.

Here's another example to try.

The Boy and the Book Report

Imagine that you're in the middle of giving a book report. Some kids in the back of the room are shooting rubber bands. The teacher tells them to stop, but it's made you lose your place and you stumble over your words.

What do you tell yourself about what happened? (Thoughts)

a) Those boys are always causing trouble.

b) They think my report is stupid and boring.

c) Why does stuff like this always happen to me?

d) Other possibilities?

How do you feel? (Feelings)

a) Annoyed

b) Sad, embarrassed

c) Frustrated

d) Other possibilities

What do you do? (Behavior)

a) Find my place quickly and keep going with report. Don't let it bother me.

b) My cheeks get hot and red. It takes me a while to get going.

c) Let out a loud sigh.

d) Other possibilities?

Have your child come up with her own scenarios. Can he think of an example from his school day?

It can also help to diagram situations that come up in your child's day to day life, putting on paper all the various pieces of the puzzle.

For example, one of the scenarios for the boy giving the book report listed above could look like this:

THOUGHTS, FEELINGS, AND BEHAVIOR

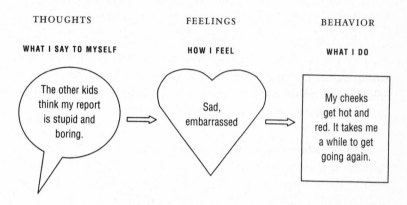

THOUGHTS	FEELINGS	BEHAVIOR
WHAT I SAY TO MYSELF	HOW I FEEL	WHAT I DO
The other kids think my report is stupid and boring.	Sad, embarrassed	My cheeks get hot and red. It takes me a while to get going again.

At this point, you're not trying to have your child alter any of his or her thoughts or feelings. This is simply an exercise in monitoring those thoughts and feelings, developing the good habit of putting pen to paper. In addition, with practice, your child will begin to see the importance of thoughts—how they give rise to feelings and behavior. But making these connections will take time. On page 118 we include a blank copy of this form for you to copy and use.

AUTOMATIC SELF-TALK

NOW LET'S BACKTRACK a bit and focus more specifically on the "thoughts" part of the equation. We've mentioned several times that each of us has a stream of automatic thoughts running through our mind. These thoughts are often undetectable, yet they are powerful nonetheless. It's like having background music on while you work. Most of the time you don't even notice it's on—you simply go about what you're doing. But have you ever felt that different music affects your mood or even your energy level? Perhaps also your ability to concentrate? The automatic self-talk playing in your mind can affect all of these things, and much more.

Children engage in self-talk, too. Here are some examples:

- Jenna doesn't get invited to a classmate's birthday party. She says to herself, "I'm such a dork. Nobody likes me."
- Hayden has to read out loud in class and makes several mistakes. He says to himself, "Everyone thinks I'm stupid."
- Liz trips during PE class and a few kids laugh. "No one will want to pick me for their team," she thinks.

We're sure you can see some problems in the logic of this self-talk. For one thing, Jenna, Hayden, and Liz are all making assumptions about what others are thinking that may or may not be true. Second, they're talking to themselves in global terms—*nobody* likes them or *everyone* will laugh at them. And finally, regardless of the truth or falseness of these statements, none of them are very useful. This type of self-talk does nothing to generate self-confidence or guide the child in productive action. While you and I can see these things, for the child in the situation, it's more difficult.

Tuning in to self-talk. To work with our thoughts and make them more adaptive and realistic, we first need to know what they are. We can't allow our self-talk to remain background music, affecting us without knowing it.

But how can you help your child tune in to her self-talk?

One of the most helpful things you can do is have your child keep a running record of her thoughts on paper. Your child may be able to do this independently, or she made need you to record her thoughts as she dictates them.

Below is a format we've found helpful, but feel free to adapt it to your child's needs. Use any type of notebook you like and make the same headings at the top. Leave space to jot down a few words about the situation and the date so you can easily monitor your child's progress. Most important, have your child write down (or dictate to you) any thoughts she's having either in anticipation of or during a social situation. In other words, what is she telling herself? What does she fear will happen? How does she feel about it? Have your child use any of the rating tools from Chapter 5 (the 0–10 scale or the fear thermometer) to write a number in the third column to represent how he or she feels or write a few words as a description.

THOUGHT DIARY

DATE/SITUATION	THOUGHTS/WHAT I AM TELLING MYSELF	HOW UPSET DO I FEEL?

When Jenna wasn't invited to the birthday party, her thought diary might have looked like this.

THOUGHT DIARY

DATE/SITUATION	THOUGHTS/WHAT I AM TELLING MYSELF	HOW UPSET DO I FEEL?
Tuesday. Overheard other girls talking about getting invites in the mail.	I'm such a dork. Nobody likes me. I don't have any friends. What's wrong with me? Everyone knows I wasn't invited and knows what a loser I am. The other girls will laugh at me. I won't be able to take it. I'll start crying and fall apart.	Very sad and hurt. 9 on feeling thermometer

Some kids have a much easier time with this task than others. Just do what you can to have your child write or dictate to you his or her thoughts as soon as possible after an upsetting event. That's when the thoughts are the freshest and the easiest to tune in to.

Some children may resist this step. They may be perfectionists and fear writing down the "wrong" thing. Reassure your child that there are no right or wrong, good or bad thoughts. Thoughts are simply thoughts.

Your child may tell you, "I don't know what I'm thinking." This is okay, too. Get in the habit of writing in the thought diary anyway. Have your child write, "I don't know what I'm thinking but I wonder if it could be . . ." For some children, you might need to offer a small incentive in the beginning of the process, at least until they catch on to the idea and realize it's not that difficult.

NOT SO GREAT EXPECTATIONS

RECALL IN CHAPTER 2 that we said your child's expectations play a sizable role in keeping him or her locked in the social anxiety spiral. A 1996 research study conducted by the psychologist Edna Foa, noted for her research on anxiety disorders, illustrates this. Foa and a colleague compared individuals with and without social phobia, focusing on their expectations regarding various social events. They asked the participants questions about the probability of something happening to them, such as someone not saying hello. They also asked the participants what they thought the consequences would be if this event actually occured.

The socially anxious people overestimated both the probability and severity of negative social events. They expected negative social events to be more likely to occur and the consequences of these events to be more severe. But these differences were found only when they were asked about social events, not other situations.

In addition, Foa's research demonstrated that one of the best predictors of "treatment outcome"—the extent to which people improve with treatment—is whether they modify their estimates of the consequences of negative social events. Those individuals who learn that unpleasant social situations aren't the end of the world, and that they can cope with such situations if they occur, are the ones who make the most progress.

Although this study was conducted using adults, our clinical experience tells us that children make the same kind of probability and severity distortions. We've also found that many children are capable of understanding these basic concepts and benefit from learning strategies to revise their expectations.

What are the odds? To address the issue of probability, we ask children to take an example from their thought diary and estimate how likely it would be that it would occur. For many children, we use the rating scale below.

What are the odds of _____ **occurring?**
(what you expect/fear will happen)

0%	10%	20%	30%	40%	50%	60%	70%	80%	90%	100%
not a chance		not likely			fifty-fifty chance			pretty sure		for sure will happen

At this point, tell your child to let his "fear do the talking." Many children write down what they think they *should* rather than what they truly believe unless you give them this instruction.

Jenna rated the chance of her experiencing disapproval from her friends—of them laughing at her and thinking she is a loser—to be about 90 percent. In other words, she was fairly certain that not getting invited to the birthday party would result in some sort of disapproval.

How bad would it be? To address severity distortions, we have children do the same thing, but this time rate how bad it would be if the situation actually occurred.

How bad would it be if _____ occurred?

(what you expect/fear will happen)

0%	10%	20%	30%	40%	50%	60%	70%	80%	90%	100%
no		not a			moderately			horrible		freaking
problem		big deal			terrible					out

Jenna thought it would be somewhere between "horrible" and "freaking out" if the situation occurred as she expected, that is, if her friends disapproved of her and she "fell apart" and began crying.

REVISING THOUGHTS AND EXPECTATIONS

ONCE YOUR CHILD becomes comfortable identifying and recording her thoughts, as well as rating her estimates of probability and severity, the next step is gently to help her challenge these ideas. The goal is to help your child see that there are many different ways she can think about a situation. Some ways can make her more worried, but other ways can make her more relaxed.

Go back to "The Girls by the Swings" and "The Boy and the Book Report." Review with your child the several different ways of viewing these situations.

Next, look over some of the entries in your child's thought diary. Again, give lots of verbal encouragement to your child for tuning in to her thoughts and recording them. Tell her that now you're going to help her see if she can think of any other possible ways to think about the situations she wrote about. Tell her that the goal of this step is to help her feel better—less worried and anxious. Be sure to proceed carefully, making sure your child doesn't perceive you as criticizing her thoughts.

In his book *Helping Your Anxious Child,* the psychologist Ronald Rapee calls this step detective thinking. Like a detective, you want your child to hunt for clues and try to figure out if the thought is actually "true" or not. We like the concept of detective thinking. It makes sense to kids of all ages and makes the process more fun.

For young children, we've developed Bailey the Bloodhound to help them in their detective thinking. Bloodhounds are known for their ability to sniff out clues. They often work with detectives and police officers to solve tough cases. We tell kids that Bailey is going to help them figure out if there are other ways to think about situations, ways that might make them feel better. We include a "Bailey the Bloodhound Detective Thinking Worksheet" on page 121. For older kids and teens, who may not think Bailey is cool, we also include a version without Bailey on page 123.

What tools does a good detective use? One is quite simple yet highly effective: questions. By asking key questions, detectives figure out if something makes sense. In other words, they figure out solutions to problems.

Here are some questions that a good detective or Bailey the Bloodhound might ask:

1. What proof is there that _____ would happen, or that _____ is true?

2. If _____ did happen, how bad would it be?

3. How do I know that the other kids would think _____ of me?

4. If they did think _____ of me, does that mean I'm really so terrible?

5. Have I run across any similar situations in the past? If so, what happened then? Was it as bad as I thought it would be?

6. Have other kids been through a similar situation?

7. How did they handle it?

8. Are there any other clues that I should consider in this situation?

Let's go back to Jenna and her thought diary.

THOUGHT DIARY

DATE/SITUATION	THOUGHTS/WHAT AM I TELLING MYSELF?	HOW UPSET DO I FEEL?
Tuesday. Overheard other girls talking about getting invites in the mail	I'm such a dork. Nobody likes me. I don't have any friends. What's wrong with me? Everyone knows I wasn't invited and knows what a loser I am. The other girls will laugh at me. I won't be able to take it. I'll start crying and fall apart.	Very sad and hurt. 9 on feeling thermometer

Her mother helped her go through the above questions, and here's what they came up with.

1. What proof is there that the girls will laugh would happen, or that nobody likes me is true? *I really don't have any proof that nobody likes me. Naomi is my friend. She likes me. Veronica is my friend, too. I guess there are some girls who like me. Maybe I'm not the most popular girl in the class, but that doesn't mean that nobody likes me. I don't actually know if the other girls will laugh at me because I wasn't invited. I think some of them will, but they're the snobby girls anyway.*

2. If the above did happen, how bad would it be? *I wouldn't like it one bit if people laughed at me. But I know that Naomi and Veronica wouldn't laugh at me. I don't know if they were invited to the party. They may not have been invited, either.*

3. How do I know that the other kids would think I'm a loser? *I'm not sure if the other girls in my class would think*

I'm a loser. I guess they might think something else, or they might not think anything at all.

4. If they did think that I'm a loser, does that mean I'm really so terrible? *Hey, if anyone thinks I'm a loser because I didn't get invited to one party, I don't need her as my friend.*

5. Have I run across any similar situations in the past? If so, what happened then? Was it as bad as I thought it would be? *I can't remember a time when this happened before.*

6. Have other kids been through a similar situation? *Probably, but I've never heard anyone talk about it before. I guess it's not something you go around advertising.*

7. How did they handle it? *I don't know.*

8. Are there any other clues that I should consider in this situation? *Maybe the girl's mother put a limit on the number of people she could invite to the party. Maybe it wasn't really because I'm a dork and a loser.*

We're not saying that this process was smooth sailing. It looks easy on paper, but Jenna and her mom spent considerable time and effort coming up with alternative ways of looking at the situation. And first, Jenna's mother had to do some good empathic listening (see Chapter 3 for a review) to let Jenna "vent" and get out her hurt and frustration. Only once Jenna's feelings were heard and validated was she open to looking at her thoughts and possible alternative ways of viewing the situation. Feel free to work on these questions in bits and pieces, giving your child plenty of time to process the information during your breaks.

After you've done the detective work as best you can, ask your child to rate her feelings again on the feeling thermometer. Ideally, the temperature will go down as your child's thoughts become more realistic. After Jenna went through this process, she re-rated her feelings at 4—quite a change and much more manage-able than her previous rating of 9. In addition, have your child re-rate her estimates of "What are the odds?" and "How bad would it be?" By going through the detective worksheet, Jenna had decided there was perhaps a fifty–fifty chance that the girls would laugh at her for not being invited to the party, but she felt as if she could handle that. Her severity rating ("How bad would it be?") dropped to 20 percent ("not a big deal").

DEVELOPING A COPING STATEMENT

SO FAR, YOU'VE helped your child understand why thoughts are important (they influence how we feel and behave), and you've de-veloped a practice of helping your child monitor his or her thoughts. In addition, you've gone through the process of asking questions related to thoughts and expectations, determining whether there might be other, more helpful ways of looking at the situation.

The next step is to help your child summarize this information into a "coping statement." We frequently do this with adults, and we've found that it works well with many children, too. Coping statements are simple and brief to-the-point reminders that the situ-ation usually isn't the calamity it's been built up to be in your child's mind. For an older child or adolescent, you can write the coping statement(s) on an index card that he or she can carry and refer to frequently throughout the day. For a younger kid, it will probably need to be only a short phrase reminding him or her to stay calm and breathe.

Generally, coping statements have two parts:

1. What will really happen
2. How to cope

Jenna's, coping card might look something like this:

Most girls won't laugh at me or think I'm a loser. If anyone does think that, it doesn't mean it's true. Everyone doesn't have to like me.

How exactly do you have your child use his coping card? You can have your child repeat his coping statement to himself when he feels anxious. This interrupts the automatic negative thoughts he's having. In addition, repeating the coping statement gives your child a healthier interpretation of the situation. Some kids even use their coping statement along with the deep-breathing techniques we presented in Chapter 5. For example, as your child inhales, he says part of the coping statement to himself, and as he exhales, he says the rest of the statement. Obviously, this works best with very brief coping statements.

Your child is likely to object, "I'm not going to remember to use my coping statement when I'm nervous. I can't think straight at those times." It's true that reassuring thoughts can be hard to summon the closer you get to an anxiety-producing situation. That's why it's important to compose a relatively brief statement and have your child memorize it, if possible. And of course, depending on the situation, your child can pull out the coping card and review the statement for a mini–coping refresher course.

BASIC BELIEFS

DEEP DOWN INSIDE, everyone has ideas about how he or she should look or act or feel. These basic beliefs are the underlying principles that give rise to your thoughts and feelings, especially those that come to your mind automatically. As we discussed in this chapter, however, monitoring thoughts and challenging expectations causes you to confront these basic beliefs. This is critical to make deep and lasting progress in overcoming social anxiety.

Below are some common beliefs of people with social anxiety. After each belief, we include some examples with which your child may identify. Go through this list with your child and see if any ring true.

- *My worth depends upon my accomplishments.*
    - I'd better get all A's or I'm no good.
    - If I'm not great in sports, other kids won't like me.
- *Anxiety and fear equal weakness.*
    - It's not cool to show you're nervous.
    - Never let them see you sweat.
    - If people know I'm nervous, they'll think I'm a wimp.
    - I have to be tough.
- *I cannot function when I am anxious.*
    - If my hands are shaking, I won't be able to give my book report.
    - I feel nervous that everyone is watching me. I'm going to strike out at my next at-bat.
- *Everyone must like me or it's horrible.*
    - If the popular kids don't like me, I'm for sure a loser.
- *I cannot tolerate criticism or rejection.*
    - I didn't get a part in the play. I'm such a failure.

Beliefs are the general assumptions that guide you through life. They represent judgments about yourself and people in general. You can see how your beliefs influence what you expect to happen in each specific situation you encounter. If your beliefs are unrealistic, your expectations will be inaccurate. In other words, unrealistic beliefs lead you to expect more "danger" than there actually is. When you enter a social situation expecting bad things to happen, the thoughts you experience won't be very helpful—that is, they will make you feel uncomfortable and distract you from the task at hand.

We don't expect you to explain all these nuances about thoughts, expectations, and beliefs to your child. They would probably just confuse him or her. But they can help you to understand how the various mental components of social anxiety disorder fit together.

Unrealistic Beliefs (about yourself and others)

Example: If I don't give a perfect oral report, the other kids will think I'm stupid. I can't stand it when other kids think bad things about me.

↓

Inaccurate Expectations (about a specific situation)

Example: The other kids will for sure notice me stumbling over my words during my report, and it will be a disaster.

↓

Maladaptive Thoughts (while in the situation)

Example: The kids can see I'm nervous. I'm doing terribly. It's all over.

A LOOK AHEAD

BY GOING THROUGH the steps in this chapter, your child should be well on the road to revising his or her thinking patterns in a more

realistic direction. You've both worked hard, so congratulate your-
selves! Now you're ready to proceed to the next chapter where we
describe another powerful set of techniques to use in the process of
conquering fear—that of "exposure."

THOUGHTS, FEELINGS, AND BEHAVIOR

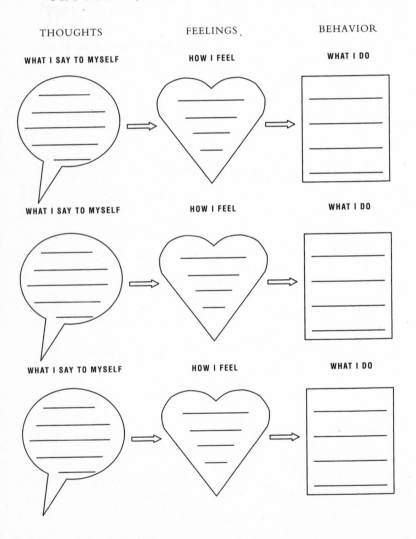

Bailey wants to know what you are thinking.

10. Out of Control! Ballistic!
9. Can't Handle It.
8. Really Tough.
7. Pretty Tough.
6. Getting Tough.
5. Not too Good.
4. Starting to Bother.
3. Just a Little Uneasy.
2. A Little Twinge.
1. Piece of Cake!

THOUGHT DIARY

DATE/SITUATION	THOUGHTS/WHAT I AM TELLING MYSELF	HOW UPSET DO I FEEL?

THOUGHT DIARY

DATE/SITUATION	THOUGHTS/WHAT I AM TELLING MYSELF	HOW UPSET DO I FEEL?

**BAILEY THE BLOODHOUND
DETECTIVE THINKING
WORKSHEET**

1. What proof is there that _____ would happen, or that _____ is true?

_____

_____

_____

_____

2. If _____ did happen, how bad would it be?

_____

_____

_____

_____

3. How do I know that the other kids would think _____ of me?

_____

_____

_____

_____

4. If they did think _____ of me, does that mean I'm really so terrible?

_____

_____

_____

_____

5. Have I run across any similar situations in the past? If so, what happened then? Was it as bad as I thought it would be?

_____

_____

_____

_____

6. Have other kids been through a similar situation?

_____

_____

_____

_____

7. How did they handle it?

_____

_____

_____

_____

8. Are there any other clues that I should consider in this situation?

_____

_____

_____

_____

DETECTIVE THINKING WORKSHEET

1. What proof is there that _____ would happen, or that _____ is true?

_____

_____

_____

_____

2. If _____ did happen, how bad would it be?

_____

_____

_____

_____

3. How do I know that the other kids would think _____ of me?

_____

_____

_____

_____

4. If they did think _____ of me, does that mean I'm really so terrible?

_____

_____

_____

_____

5. Have I run across any similar situations in the past? If so, what happened then? Was it as bad as I thought it would be?

_____

_____

_____

_____

6. Have other kids been through a similar situation?

_____

_____

_____

_____

7. How did they handle it?

_____

_____

_____

_____

8. Are there any other clues that I should consider in this situation?

_____

_____

_____

_____

CHAPTER 7

Facing the Fear

*The Principles of "Exposure Therapy"
Made Kid-Friendly*

W E'VE ALL heard the advice: If you fall off a horse, get right back on or fear will set in. In many cases, this makes good sense. For instance, when a friend of mine totaled her car in an accident a few years ago, she didn't want to drive again. She was quite shook up, and she worried that something else bad might happen. Although her hesitancy and anxiety were understandable, I encouraged her to begin driving again as soon as possible. The longer she waited, the more difficult it would be.

Facing your fears can be powerful, especially when you stay in the situation long enough to learn that you *can* cope and that a catastrophe isn't likely to occur. This process is called *exposure* or *exposure therapy*. Most clinical research studies have shown that to reduce fear and anxiety, the treatment process must include an exposure component. You can't simply sit in a therapist's office exploring how and why you developed your fears; you have to confront them head-on.

Exposure works exceedingly well for simple phobias, such as a fear of snakes or a fear of heights, and it can prove effective for other anxiety disorders. Unfortunately, it's not so clear-cut in the case of social fears. Social situations are different each time, so it can be difficult to build up the repeated exposures necessary to conquer your fears.

In this chapter, we first explain in more detail what exposure is and why some experts think it works. Then we show you ways to coach your child using these techniques, paying special attention to the nuances of applying exposure methods to social anxiety. Despite the unique challenges you might face in using exposure methods with your child, we believe you'll find it's worth the extra effort. There's often no better way to make significant and lasting changes in your child's social comfort level.

A SIMPLE EXAMPLE OF EXPOSURE THERAPY

WHEN I FIRST explain exposure therapy to my socially anxious clients—regardless of their age—I almost always use the treatment of a simple phobia as an example. This makes it easier for them to understand the basic principles involved, to see how exposure works in its ideal form. From there I show them how to adapt these principles to fit their situation. We follow the same format in this chapter, first describing the basics of what exposure is and what makes it work. We then show you how to introduce these concepts to your child, making them kid-friendly.

Eight-year-old Debbie's parents brought her to see me because of a variety of anxiety problems. For the purposes of this discussion, we'll limit our focus to her fear of heights. Debbie had difficulty going into tall buildings and walking across bridges, especially if she looked down. But the main thing Debbie wanted to work on was being able to climb on the playground equipment, especially the monkey bars. That is what most of the girls her age did during recess, and she felt terrible not being able to participate. Although Debbie had more serious anxiety problems, this is the one that bothered her the most, so we worked on it. The principles she'd learn dealing with her height phobia would later transfer to the other areas we'd need to tackle.

I spent the first session with Debbie and her parents getting a good feel for her situation. Apparently she had once seen someone fall off a slide, and this experience stuck with her and generalized to a fear of heights. Now when she encountered any type of situation involving heights, she felt dizzy and short of breath. Her heart also "felt like it was coming out of her chest," as she put it. The physical sensations intensified the higher she was. Although Debbie's muscles were plenty strong and she had no difficulty with balance or coordination, she feared the monkey bars the most, worrying that she might fall.

During the second session I provided Debbie and her parents with a rationale for exposure therapy and taught Debbie some breathing techniques. They grasped the concepts quickly, and Debbie, although naturally a little apprehensive, was motivated to get to work. By the third session, we were ready to carry out her first exposure. We met at a nearby park so I could go over the procedures with them. Later, her parents coached her themselves.

Debbie and I picked the fourth rung of the ladder on the monkey bars to begin the process. We estimated that this level would arouse her anxiety to a moderate degree without completely overwhelming her. Starting slowly would increase Debbie's chances for success, making her feel more confident to move to the next level.

The first time, I climbed alongside her. We stayed on the rung for a little while, and I asked Debbie to rate her anxiety on a scale of 0 to 10, with 0 being completely relaxed and 10 being the most scared she'd ever been. She rated her level at 6. Interestingly, despite her feeling anxious on the inside, she appeared calm (other than clutching the bars rather tightly). I pointed this out to her and she was surprised. "I thought all the other kids would be able to tell how scared I am," she said.

As we continued working our way up the rungs of the ladder, I periodically asked Debbie to rate her anxiety level. Her level predictably rose to 6 or 7 with each higher step, yet dropped off to 3 or 4 as we remained there for a while. I coached her as we went, reminding her to focus on taking deep breaths. I also encouraged her to look around and not clutch the bars as if her life depended on it.

Next, I had Debbie repeat this entire procedure while I watched and her father served as the coach. By the time they had worked their way up the rungs of the ladder, Debbie was beaming, feeling justifiably proud of herself.

Over the course of several weeks, Debbie and her parents completed exposure sessions on their own. In addition, we met in my office to process what she was learning. I wanted to know how her thoughts were changing and how her body was reacting physically to the exposure challenges. As we've said, children can have difficulty articulating their thoughts, especially discerning changes in their thoughts. But with some help, here is a list of things we came up with that Debbie had gained from her exposure therapy:

- "I learned my body works even when I'm scared. I used to think I wouldn't be able to move when I felt so dizzy and shaky."
- "Feeling scared doesn't last forever. It goes away."
- "I can do things that I'm afraid of—it gets easier."
- "Most kids won't even notice if I'm scared."
- "If anyone notices I'm scared, it's not such a big deal."

Debbie had worked hard, and her work paid off. She was now able to play with her friends at recess. More important, she felt better about herself and was ready to begin conquering her other fears.

So why did climbing up and down the monkey bar ladder relieve Debbie's fear of heights? You've seen with her case *how* exposure works—what Debbie had to do to reduce her fear. Now let's look at *why* it works.

WHY EXPOSURE WORKS

NO ONE KNOWS for sure why exposure works, but there are two main theories. Some researchers believe in a theory called habituation, while others think exposure works primarily through cognitive

processes. From our own clinical experience, we believe that a combination of factors is involved.

The theory of habituation. One theory asserts that the more
you become accustomed to doing or seeing something, such as a situation or behavior, the more you can tolerate it. It becomes such a
part of your life—a habit—that it no longer seems like a big deal. In
the case of social fears, the occasions or other stimuli that once pro-
voked anxiety now cease to do so. Let's look at an example.

When I was in graduate school, I moved to an apartment complex
that was very close to the campus. Unfortunately, it was also right by
the airport. The airplanes were so loud when they flew overhead that
I couldn't concentrate on anything. Sometimes they startled me, and I
practically jumped from my chair. They even woke me up at night. I
had no idea how I was going to stand it.

About a week after I'd moved in, I was talking to my mother on
the phone and she commented on the noise in the background. I
hadn't even noticed. The noise of the airplanes had stopped provok-
ing any kind of reaction from me.

This is how habituation works. By repeated exposure to something, you stop reacting to it. In laboratory studies, habituation is
usually determined using physiological measures such as pulse rate
or blood pressure. When I work with clients, we instead use the same
0 to 10 ratings we've mentioned throughout the book, or the fear
thermometer for younger kids. Using the appropriate scale, clients
rate their anxiety levels at frequent intervals. In each case I can tell if
we need to adjust the exposure.

Cognitive explanations. Another theory is that exposure works
by helping you change your expectations about what will happen in
particular social situations. If all goes well with your exposures, you
learn that the chances of something awful happening are pretty slim,
and if something awful does happen, you can cope.

Of course, anyone can tell you, or you can tell yourself, "There's nothing to be afraid of." But the words are not enough. Anyone who's ever tried to tell a frightened three-year-old that there are no monsters in the closet knows the futility of mere words. You have to *show* the child it's safe by shining a flashlight in the closet, poking all around, encouraging the child to look in, and so on. For beliefs to truly change, they must be disproved on a very basic "gut" level. Proponents of the cognitive interpretation of how exposure works believe that being in the fearful situation activates one's thoughts and beliefs, thus making them amenable to change.

THE KEYS TO EFFECTIVE EXPOSURE: MAKE IT GRADUAL, REPEATED, AND PROLONGED

AS YOU CAN see from Debbie's experience, exposure therapy is not complicated, at least in the case of simple phobias. You really need to follow only three principles to maximize its effectiveness.

Don't do too much too soon. A key to successful exposure treatment is to go slowly and don't have your child take on more than he or she can handle. Obviously, exposures create some anxiety. That's necessary for habituation to take place. But don't overwhelm or terrify your child. This only makes him or her more fearful and discouraged.

The trick is to break your child's fears into a series of steps, with the first few steps being only mildly challenging and later steps increasing in difficulty. To do this, you create a hierarchy—a list of situations that elicit anxiety, rank ordered by the amount of distress each would lead to if your child entered the situation.

For Debbie's parents, constructing a hierarchy was relatively easy.

Debbie's Hierarchy

1. Climb up to the fourth rung of the ladder on the monkey bars. Do with Mom or Dad present. Continue with this step until anxiety level decreases by at least 50 percent.
2. Climb to the fifth rung of the ladder. Do with Mom or Dad present. Remain until anxiety level decreases by at least 50 percent.
3. Practice steps 1 and 2 with Mom or Dad several feet away.
4. Continue working up the ladder, each time remaining on the rung until anxiety decreases. Do first with parent near, then with parent at a distance.
5. Gradually increase time on each rung and work on relaxing grip on the bars, looking from side to side, down, etc.

Debbie's parents made some adjustments to the hierarchy as they went along, but this gave them a good initial plan to follow. Again, by starting with small steps they maximized the chances of her meeting with success early. This helped motivate her to continue, even when the exposures got a little tougher for her.

Once Debbie was able to climb to the top of the monkey bars with minimal anxiety, they made a new hierarchy to help her become comfortable hanging on the bars, swinging from bar to bar, and finally dropping to the ground safely.

Make it a habit. For exposure therapy to be successful, you need to practice consistently and frequently. If your child exposes himself to a fearful situation and then waits three months before he does it again, he's not likely to benefit much from either the first or the second experience. I usually ask people to try to practice exposures at least three times a week. Obviously, the more your child practices, the more rapidly he'll overcome his fears.

Exposures should be prolonged. How long should exposure sessions last? The usual guideline is to remain in the situation until anxiety begins to decline, preferably to a mild level. The theory is that if you leave the situation while your anxiety level is still high, it reinforces your fear and can do more harm than good. Because of this guideline, the process of completing an entire exposure session can be quite time-consuming. Many of the treatment manuals used in research studies specify ninety-minute exposure sessions.

Actually, the issue isn't the length of time per se; it's remaining in the situation long enough to realize that fear doesn't persist indefinitely, that catastrophes aren't likely to occur, and that the situation can be handled. Once your child gets going with the items on her hierarchy, you both may find that it takes progressively less time to complete an exposure session. This is because you take with you what you learned from one session to another. After Debbie had made it up several rungs of the ladder, she was familiar with the process. She was learning that her body wasn't reacting with quite the same intensity (although she wouldn't have stated it that way) and that she was more courageous than she'd given herself credit for.

SPECIAL CHALLENGES IN THE CASE
OF SOCIAL ANXIETY

BY NOW YOU have a good understanding of how exposure works in its ideal form. But as we said at the beginning of the chapter, there are special challenges to using exposure therapy for social anxiety. We describe these challenges below and then show you how to effectively work around them.

It's not always easy to develop a hierarchy. Social situations tend to be complex and unpredictable and involve many skills, all of which make it difficult to develop a hierarchy of gradual steps.

Think of all the aspects involved in a child trying to join a group of kids already playing. She must read nonverbal cues to find a good time to approach the others, perhaps ask to join in on the game or activity, make conversation, listen and show interest, and so on. Simultaneously, she must manage any physical symptoms of anxiety she's experiencing, and she may also have to cope with negative thoughts ("They don't want to play with me" or "I'm no good at . . ."). That's a lot to do at once. Add to the scenario that the child has little control over how the other kids will act. With so many unknown variables, no wonder many socially anxious children hang back instead of joining in on what could be a fun time.

Of course, there are ways to break the task of joining a group of kids or making friends into small steps. But even what seems to you to be an easy step, such as saying hi to someone on the playground, might be too challenging for some kids. In reality, creating a gradual hierarchy is not very neat and tidy in the case of many social situations.

Even if you and your child come up with a workable hierarchy, you may encounter other problems. First of all, situations may arise that your child isn't ready for—they're too high up on her hierarchy—but neither of you has any choice in the matter. Imagine that your child's teacher surprises the class by assigning an oral book report due next week. Certainly, you can try to talk with the teacher and explain the situation. Sometimes, though, you're simply stuck with switching gears on the hierarchy and having your child work on something that ideally should wait until easier items are accomplished.

On the other hand, an opportunity might come along that your child doesn't want to pass up. Maybe a girl she's been eager to get to know calls her and asks her over to play. Your daughter doesn't feel ready, but she also doesn't want to risk not being asked a second time.

With Debbie's height phobia, it was easy to follow a linear, gradual format. But trying to follow the principle of gradual exposure can be much more difficult when it comes to social situations.

Repeated exposure isn't always feasible. Another difficulty is that repeatedly having your child expose himself to the same situation isn't always possible. Some things like socializing with friends or going to birthday parties don't follow a particular schedule. You don't always have control over whether or not your child can practice his exposures three times a week.

Opportunities for things involving public speaking are even less likely to occur on a regular basis. When I was promoting my first book, *Dying of Embarrassment,* and then again with *Painfully Shy,* I did frequent radio interviews, and my anxiety significantly decreased over time. I got to the point where I could do an interview, feel few if any physical symptoms, and not obsess for days about how I sounded. I grew confident in my ability to get my ideas across, and I also didn't worry as much when I wasn't perfectly polished. It was truly a case of exposure at work; the sheer quantity and frequency of the interviews made me relax physically and mentally.

However, now that I've been in more of a writing phase again and haven't done any media appearances lately, I know I will be anxious when the time comes to do more interviews and public speaking. The good thing is that I know I'll be able to call upon my previous positive experiences and realize that I'm up to the task so that the anxiety won't overwhelm me.

There are ways to simulate situations when the actual opportunity isn't available. But in terms of the traditional guideline of repeating exposures frequently, it's not always practical.

Social situations are often brief, making prolonged exposure difficult. Remember that to habituate to something, you have to remain in the situation long enough for your anxiety level to diminish—to become more comfortable. Again, this principle can be difficult to follow. Think of all the social situations that are brief by nature: answering the phone, saying hello to someone, smiling at a neighbor on the street, raising your hand in class.

There's no way to prolong these situations so that your child's anxiety level can come down naturally. In seconds or minutes, the event is over, but your child is left with a racing heart and trembling hands. By virtue of the brief nature of the experience, your child doesn't have the opportunity to learn that the anxiety will dissipate.

Your child may also be left with doubts in his mind about how the situation went. It happened so fast and while he was so acutely anxious, it's easy to misinterpret things. In other words, your child may not get the positive shift in thoughts that comes with prolonged exposure.

USING YOUR CHILD'S IMAGINATION

THE TYPE OF exposure Debbie used to overcome her height phobia is called *in vivo* exposure. This simply means that the exposure takes place in the actual situation. Another type of exposure, *imaginal* exposure, can be very useful in reducing social fears. The procedures and principles are essentially the same; the only difference is that the exposure is carried out in your child's mind.

Imaginal exposure can sidestep many of the problems we discussed in the previous section. With imaginal exposure, you can control more of the variables that can be unpredictable in actual social situations. You can also help your child carry out exposures that are not actually available. In addition, imaginal exposure can help your child prepare to complete exposures in real life.

How can you and your child implement imaginal exposure? Just as with in vivo exposure, the first step is to develop a hierarchy. Then, for each step on the hierarchy, you and your child create a scene—actually write a "script" to describe it. Work with your child to include as many details as possible about the situation, especially about the things your child fears will happen. Include any troubling physical sensations your child experiences, thoughts your child has, other people's reactions, and so on.

Then, for each step of the hierarchy, have your child imagine the scenario. You may read the script aloud or record it onto a tape. Some people buy loop tapes in which the tape repeats over and over. Regardless of how you go about it, the goal is to have your child imagine the scene, allow himself to become fully immersed in it, and experience the accompanying anxiety. Encourage your child to stay with the scene for however long it takes for the anxiety to subside.

While doing imaginal or any other type of exposure, remind your child to use the breathing techniques we presented in Chapter 5. This can make the process more manageable. You can also have your child use a simple coping statement such as, "I can do it." Just make sure the coping statement doesn't become a distraction from imagining the scene. If your child doesn't pay attention to the exposure, it won't have a chance to work.

IT'S YOUR TURN

NOW THAT YOU have a good idea of how and why exposure works, you can go through the process with your child. We'll walk you through it, step by step.

Explain the concept of exposure to your child. As we mentioned at the outset of this chapter, we find that the easiest way to explain exposure therapy is to begin with an example of a simple phobia—and often a height phobia works well. You can go through the example of Debbie and climbing the ladder of the monkey bars, or make up your own example.

One mother used the example of a child learning to swim. You start out slowly, first having the child become comfortable with his feet in the water and perhaps splashing around. Gradually, you walk with the child into the water more and more, showing the child that it is fun to get wet and splash around. In contrast, you wouldn't throw the child into the deep end. That would not only be dangerous, it would scare the child and make him never want to go into the water again.

Similarly, you want to reassure your child that you're not going to ask him to do anything drastic or overwhelming, something that he's not ready for. You're going to start slow—on a low rung of the ladder. You'll climb higher on the ladder only as your child gets comfortable on the lower rungs.

Explain to your child that you'll be coming up with steps for him to take to overcome his fears. Again, reassure him that the steps will start out easy and that you'll be coaching him all the way.

Develop hierarchy items. After you've explained the concept of exposure to your child, the next step is actually to generate the items for the hierarchy—each of the steps (rungs) of the ladder. The best place to begin this task is to refer back to the goal and list of objectives you completed in Chapter 4. Take the objectives you wrote down and think of specific examples of each one. What particular situations do you want your child to enter? What do you want your child to do once he or she gets there?

Objectives are stated in general terms that let you know when you've achieved your goal; hierarchy items are much more concrete and detailed, describing specific behaviors and specific settings. Each description should be detailed enough so that if your child attempted an exposure right now, you'd know exactly where to go, what to do, with whom he or she would be interacting, and so on.

Remember Corey, the fifteen-year-old with the fear of public speaking? (You can look back at pages 73–75.) One of his objectives was to "ask questions and express my opinion during classes." Let's use his example to see how the process of coming up with hierarchy items works.

Corey needed to think of specific examples for this objective, things he might actually be able to do for his exposures. Using his knowledge about his classes and their typical format, here are some hierarchy items he created:

- Ask one question during history class
- Offer a comment during literature class
- Agree to work a math problem on the board

Do you see how these are all very specific examples of his more general objective?

Keep in mind that each hierarchy item you develop is likely to bring on a different level of anxiety. For example, Corey was much less afraid to ask a question than he was to offer his opinion. Don't worry at this point about precisely how much anxiety each exposure will bring on. We take on the task of ranking the feared situations next. Right now, just concentrate on helping your child develop a complete list of exposure ideas for each objective you set in Chapter 4. Involve your child in this process as much or as little as you feel is appropriate.

Create the hierarchy. Now that you have a list of hierarchy items, the next step is to put them in order of difficulty. Ask your child to rate (using the 0–10 scale or the fear thermometer) how difficult each task would be if he was actually to complete the exposure right now.

Sometimes this is a difficult concept for children to grasp. If so, have your child rate the items according to a low, medium, or high level of difficulty. A low-challenge exposure is one that would likely elicit an anxiety level of 0–3, a medium-challenge exposure would probably bring on an anxiety level of 4–7, while a high-challenge exposure would peak at an anxiety level of 8–10. Another way you can do this task is to write each item on an index card. Then have your child order the cards in terms of how hard each would be.

Start with the easiest item on the hierarchy. You're ready to begin helping your child face his or her fears. Begin with the lowest item on the hierarchy, the one that will evoke the least amount of anxiety. Have your child do whatever the task is or enter the situation. If you're doing the exposures in vivo, the child completes the exposure in real life. In contrast, if you're starting with imaginal exposure, your child listens to a tape describing the scene.

Just like Debbie on the monkey bars, your child's anxiety level will rise. This is normal and to be expected. Your child may visibly show distress and possibly even beg you to end the exposure. Try not to do this. If you allow your child to quit, you'll reinforce the child's belief that he can't do it. Encourage your child to stay with it, even if it gets tough. Only by staying in the situation until the anxiety naturally subsides will your child learn

- I can do this.
- Anxiety doesn't last forever.
- My anxiety doesn't control me.
- It isn't so bad.

Repeat the process for each item on the hierarchy. Follow this procedure for each item on the hierarchy. Remember, it may take weeks or even months to go through an entire hierarchy. Refer to Chapter 3 and Chapter 4 for tips on motivating your child. Your child may need incentives and small rewards to complete the items on the hierarchy. This is okay and perfectly understandable. Think about how you'd react if someone asked you to do the very thing you're most afraid of. Most of us wouldn't be too thrilled and would need a lot of encouragement.

You'll likely need to create more than one hierarchy for the different goals you set in Chapter 4. The nice thing is, after you and your child have gone through this process once, it gets easier. This is because what your child learns by going through one hierarchy generalizes to the next. In addition, your child is gaining confidence all the time and is ready to take on increasingly more difficult challenges.

TIPS FOR SUCCESSFUL EXPOSURE

LET'S GO OVER some tips to make your child's exposure therapy as successful as possible.

- Don't dive in too fast. It's better to include many manageable situations for the lower rungs of the hierarchy.
- You may need to repeat items on the hierarchy. Doing the exposure once isn't enough. Before you have your child move on to the next item, make sure that he could repeat the exposure without major difficulty. If your child feels he's barely survived the exposure, it's not time to move on. He doesn't have to be perfectly relaxed to say he's mastered an exposure, but he should be relatively comfortable.
- Try to have your child stay in the fear-producing situation until her anxiety level begins to drop. If your child stops the exposure while her anxiety level is still at a peak level or climbing, she doesn't experience the inevitable reduction of symptoms and confidence boost that occur in any tough situation, given enough time.
- Have your child make use of coping techniques during exposures, such as deep breathing and positive self-talk.
- Help your child evaluate his progress constructively. Many kids minimize their efforts, saying, "Well, most kids could already do what I just did. It's no big deal." Gently challenge this type of thinking. You might say something like, "So what if some other kids can do this? This is tough for you, and you're working hard to overcome your fears. You deserve credit for your courage."

GIVE YOURSELF CREDIT, TOO

GIVE YOURSELF A lot of credit for your hard work as well. It's a tough job being the coach. Although your child is the one actually entering the feared situations, it can be almost as difficult watching, knowing what your child is going through. Know that exposure therapy, however hard it is, will yield rich rewards for your child—a life not controlled by fear.

Learning Social Skills

The ABCs of Making Friends and Acting Assertively

S HY AND anxious children who frequently avoid or withdraw from social situations may not develop the social skills they need. Amy is eleven years old and has been going through treatment for social anxiety disorder for several months. She has learned to manage many of her anxious thoughts and physical reactions, and now she wants to socialize more with other kids. The problem is that she's been on the outskirts of things for so long she doesn't know how to go about such basic things as talking with others in the hallway, sitting with kids at lunch, or inviting friends over.

Fortunately, social skills can be learned. Ideally, the groundwork is laid early in childhood through the natural course of playing with other children. However, it's never too late. Even children like Amy, who have up to this point remained in the background of the social landscape, can acquire the knack for warming up and joining in with others. In this chapter, we show you how to coach your child to success in this most important area.

WHAT ARE SOCIAL SKILLS?

SOCIAL SKILLS ARE what educators and psychologists call the group of behaviors needed to relate to others in an effective manner. Social skills include

- listening
- starting and maintaining a conversation
- asking questions or asking for help
- giving and receiving compliments
- introducing yourself or other people
- joining in with others

Social skills also involve the nonverbal aspect of communication such as body language and eye contact.

Children master and express social skills differently at various ages. For example, an important social skill is joining an ongoing interaction. A toddler may successfully do this by reaching out his arms or calling out to gain attention. This is appropriate for a child this age. For an elementary school child, the same skill might be expressed by saying, "Hi! Can I play, too?"

We all need basic social competencies to successfully navigate our world. Yet not every child must be a social butterfly. Your child can be naturally quiet and reserved and still function effectively in the social realm.

Note that some children with social anxiety disorder actually have adequate social skills, they simply don't apply them in certain situations. Their anxiety overwhelms them and causes them to freeze. Despite knowing what to do, their social skills remain rusty from lack of practice. In contrast, other children with social anxiety disorder have not acquired adequate social skills in the first place. Whatever case holds true, this chapter shows you how to help your child join in on the fun of childhood.

DEVELOPING AND IMPROVING SOCIAL SKILLS

IT IS HEARTBREAKING to watch your child hover on the outskirts of a group of kids playing. You want so much for him to join in with the others, to fit in and be accepted. What can you do to help?

Step 1: Determine your child's social strengths and weaknesses. The first thing you need to do is determine what social skills your child already possesses. Below is a checklist for you to complete. Go through the list and check whether each item *usually* applies to your child. Your child doesn't necessarily have to display the skill every day for you to check the item, but it should be a natural behavior, not one that causes your child a great deal of dread. Consider asking your child's teacher to complete a checklist, as well.

Social Skills Attributes Checklist

- ❑ Approaches others positively
- ❑ Expresses wishes and preferences clearly
- ❑ Asserts own rights and needs appropriately
- ❑ Is not easily intimidated by bullies
- ❑ Expresses frustrations and anger effectively and without harming others or property
- ❑ Gains access to ongoing groups at play and work
- ❑ Enters ongoing discussions on the subject; makes relevant contributions to ongoing activities
- ❑ Takes turns fairly easily
- ❑ Shows interest in others; exchanges information with and requests information from others appropriately
- ❑ Negotiates and compromises with others appropriately
- ❑ Does not draw inappropriate attention to self

❏ Accepts and enjoys peers and adults of ethnic groups other than his or her own

❏ Interacts nonverbally with other children with smiles, waves, nods, etc.

From Diane E. McClellan and Lilian G. Katz, *"Young Children's Social Development,"* an *ERIC Digest*.

Step 2: Experiment and practice with social skills. Now that you have a good idea of what social skills your child needs to work on, the next step is to experiment and practice with the skill. There are many ways you can do this.

One way you can help your child with social skills is through play. Do you have some puppets you can use? (You can make basic puppets with a sock and a colored marker, or you can use stuffed animals instead.) Each of you selects a puppet to be and then acts out different social situations. Does your child have trouble expressing his or her needs? Role-play with the puppets, letting your child ask the teacher a question, such as, "May I use the restroom, please?" Obviously, for older kids you wouldn't use puppets, but you could still role-play the situation. You may need to begin with you being the one asking the question so your child can see how you do it. This sounds like a simple task, but for many socially anxious kids, drawing attention to themselves by asking questions is scary and uncomfortable.

You may need to provide direct instructions on how to perform the skill. For example, if your child is reluctant to use the telephone (many children with social anxiety have a phone phobia), he might not know how to greet his friends' parents if they answer the phone, or ask to speak to his friend. He may not know how to leave a message on an answering machine, and so on. Have your child listen when you call someone on the phone. Then discuss the different aspects of what you did. After you've provided some how-to information, role-play different phone call situations with your child.

Be gentle as you provide feedback to your child. She's probably self-conscious as it is. If you come on too strongly with what she did incorrectly, she's likely to resist your further attempts at helping her. One thing you can do in a role play is do something wrong on purpose. For example, if you're practicing holding a conversation, deliberately avoid eye contact and speak in a quiet tone of voice. Ask your child to tell you what you could have done differently. This makes it a little less threatening. Feel free to be silly. Make it into a game. A little humor goes a long way toward gaining your child's interest and cooperation.

There are also books for children on topics such as making friends and handling conflict (see the Resources section). Read one of these books with your child and talk about it afterward. You can also gain some valuable information about social skills from watching television with your child. We particularly enjoy and find helpful some of the old classics, such as *Leave It to Beaver* and *The Andy Griffith Show*. The characters on these shows frequently encounter social "challenges," and this can be a good starting point for discussions with your child.

Make your practice sessions short. Try to maintain a spirit of, "Hey, let's try this and see what happens," as you and your child act out different social situations. When your child becomes comfortable practicing social skills with you, branch out and have your child practice with a sibling, the other parent, or a friend with whom he or she feels comfortable.

Step 3: Apply the social skill in real-life situations. Next you need to have your child start practicing her social skills in real-life situations. Keep all the principles for successful exposure in mind (see the previous chapter) as you're doing this. For example, start slow and easy. If your child has difficulty making eye contact, don't expect her to maintain a ten-minute witty conversation with a neighbor right off the bat. Give lots of praise for effort and don't expect perfection. Remember, we're not trying to change your child's personality. Rather, we want to increase her skills to the point where she feels confident enough to get her needs met, be a part of a group, and simply have a good time.

GENERAL SUGGESTIONS FOR PARENTS

THE BASIC THREE-STEP process above is the crux of social skill training: (1) identify social strengths and weaknesses, (2) practice and experiment with social skills, and (3) apply the skills in real-life situations. Next we share some general suggestions of things to keep in mind as you're working with your child on developing good social skills.

Give your child plenty of practice socializing. Invite other children to play at your house. Children often feel more comfortable on their own turf. Sometimes shy children are more relaxed playing with slightly younger children, so this is also an option to try. Have the time period be fairly brief at first and try to have an activity planned you know your child enjoys.

Take your child to places where he can be around other children, even if he chooses not to talk to anyone. Your local library may have a children's story hour; go to the park when the weather allows. Again, don't force your child to interact but arrange for outings that make socializing possible.

A special challenge occurs when one or both parents are shy themselves. If this is the case for you, providing opportunities for your child to socialize may seem completely out of the question. This was the case for Abby, but she found a way around her problem by enlisting the help of relatives.

Abby found it difficult to provide her ten-year-old son, Jacob, with the amount of socializing he needed. Jacob wasn't having problems socially. In fact, he thrived on being around other people. But Abby was quiet, had few friends, and found it extremely difficult to initiate things with other people. She was working in therapy to become more outgoing—for Jacob's sake as well as her own—but she still had a long way to go.

"It was so easy when he was little and all he needed was to be fed, held, changed, and kissed. I was good at that," she explained. "But now Jacob's at the age where he wants to be around other people. Just being with me isn't very exciting."

Fortunately, Abby's sister-in-law, Rhonda, was quite outgoing and had a busy household with four children. There were always neighborhood kids coming and going, and she told Abby she wouldn't mind one more child being around. They worked out an arrangement where Jacob went to Rhonda's house a few times a week after school. This worked out great. Abby spent the time at therapy and doing her exposures, and Jacob was content to play with his cousins more often.

This type of arrangement can also work with neighbors. Look around to see where several children are playing out in the yard. We know it is difficult, but if you could become acquainted with an outgoing mom in the neighborhood, it might be a wonderful opportunity for your child to socialize with different people and become exposed to different personality styles.

Break social events into small, manageable pieces. Sometimes new social situations can be daunting for children because the whole thing seems huge and overwhelming. If possible, break the event into smaller pieces that your child can relate to. For example, Eric's son, Collin, was nervous about his first den meeting for Cub Scouts. Collin had no idea what to expect, and the images he formed in his mind were frightening, not to mention way off base. Eric was able to reassure Collin with the following pieces of information, which broke the meeting up into smaller, more familiar pieces:

- "Remember the time you played at Derick's house? The meeting will be at his house and you'll probably have a little time to play before the meeting, just like you did the other time you were there. I bet he has some neat stuff."
- "You've met Derick's parents before. They seem pretty nice. His dad is the den leader. He'll be there to tell both of us what we're going to do."
- "We'll probably sing some songs, play a game, and eat a snack."

Collin had no idea what a den meeting was like, but he could relate to playing at Derick's house, singing songs, and eating a snack. These things were familiar to him and helped him feel less anxious about attending the meeting.

Remind your child of past success. It's also important to help children remember their previous successes and to build on those. For example, Janice was having difficulty getting her son, George, to attend Sunday school. They had joined a new church and this was going to be a new experience for him. Janice reminded George that he hadn't wanted to go to kindergarten at first, but he now enjoyed it and looked forward to it. They talked about how it had been scary for him because he didn't know the teacher or the other children. For the first few weeks, his stomach hurt in the morning and he couldn't eat any breakfast. Janice told him that what he was feeling starting Sunday school class was just like what he had gone through in the beginning of "regular" school. He might be nervous for a few weeks, but then he'd get used to it and it would be fun.

Don't do too much for your child. When you go to a restaurant, do you encourage your child to order his own food? When your child wants to have a friend over to play, do you have her call the friend herself?

It's a natural parental instinct to want to shield our children from things we know are painful or difficult. But sometimes we don't do children any favors when we take over for them. By doing so, we subtly give children the message that they're not capable of doing for themselves. In addition, they don't get the valuable practice they need.

If you realize that you've been overprotecting your child and doing too much, first of all, don't be too hard on yourself. We've all made similar mistakes. Second, don't withdraw your help all at once. This proves confusing and perhaps overwhelming to your child. Explain to your child that you think you've been doing things that he could do for himself. Give an example. Tell him that you're going to help him learn to do more things independently (such as ordering his own food) but that you're not going to expect him to be able to do so overnight.

Help your child focus on the right thing. It was the 1997 NBA finals with the Chicago Bulls facing the Utah Jazz. Superstar Michael Jordan had been sick with the flu, and Bulls fans feared the worst: Michael wouldn't play. Yet Jordan did play, winning the game for the Bulls and giving perhaps the best performance of his career.

Think of why the Bulls won the game. Jordan, fighting a fever, got out on the court. He wasn't thinking about himself or his aches and pains but instead was focusing on the task at hand—winning the basketball game. It worked, and the Bulls went on to win their fifth NBA title.

Now let's switch gears. Imagine that your child is going to a dance class for the first time. Her teacher introduces her to another new girl in the class. Your child is so focused on her own anxiety (her stomach hurts, she's feeling shaky, she's worried the class will be too hard, she thinks her outfit looks funny . . .) that she barely mumbles hello to the girl and can't keep even a brief conversation going.

Paying attention to the wrong things—in your daughter's case, her own anxiety—interferes with the task at hand. Because she was so focused on herself, she missed out on an opportunity to make a new friend.

Sometimes simply explaining this to your child helps him or her decrease this self-focus. As a rule, most shy and anxious kids are caring people who want to help others. Suggest to your child that she find someone in the group who is shy, too, and try to help her feel more comfortable.

Your child may also benefit from some basic, explicit instruction on what's helpful and what's not helpful to focus on during social situations. For example, tell your child it's not helpful to focus on any physical symptoms, such as blushing or shaking. Instead, tell him to take some deep breaths, silently say the word "relax," and redirect his focus to what the other person is doing or saying.

If your child is bothered by intrusive negative thoughts during social situations (e.g., "I'm really blowing this"), coach him to say the word "stop" or to imagine a stop sign. You want your child to interrupt these unhelpful thoughts as soon as he notices them. They don't serve any function except to distract your child from the social situation and make him feel less comfortable. In addition, when people are preoccupied with themselves (even if it's only their own anxiety), they tend to project a less than approachable image.

Teach your child persistence. When I think of persistence, I think of Andrew. Andrew was in second grade, and he loved sports. He and his father watched all kinds of sports together on television. Andrew knew all the rules, all the players, and even a lot of statistics about a variety of sports. When Andrew's father's friends were over, Andrew could talk sports right along with the rest of the guys. Unfortunately, Andrew wasn't the most athletic kid for his age. He was a bit clumsy, and he wasn't very fast.

Every day at recess the boys in his class played football outside on a big grassy field. And every day Andrew joined right in. He was frustrated, however, because no one would throw him the ball. He was often in the right place, open and ready to catch a pass, but no one would give him a chance. Andrew was pretty quiet when he was in a group. He didn't call out to the other boys that he was open or that he wanted the ball.

Every day after school Andrew told his father how much he wanted to be in on the action. "Why wouldn't the other kids pass me the ball? After all, I was open. Maybe I should quit trying and play something else by myself," he told his dad.

But Andrew didn't give up. His father worked with him on ways to get the other boys' attention. They practiced out in the backyard. Andrew's father coached him on calling out, "I'm open. Pass me the ball." Andrew's voice was too quiet at first, and his father had to encourage him to yell like he really meant it.

One day Andrew came home excited as could be. "I got my chance!" he exclaimed. "David passed me the football, and I made the play for a touchdown!" Andrew said the best part was when a boy on the other team gave him a high five and asked if he'd be on his team tomorrow.

Many times, the only thing that separates successful socializers from those waiting in the wings is persistence. Kids who aren't shy often put themselves out there, letting others know they want to be included, they want to play. They keep asking in one way or another until they succeed in becoming a part of the group. This obviously doesn't come naturally for shy kids, so, like Andrew's father, you'll have to encourage your child to keep at it.

DEALING WITH THE NOT-SO-NICE

ALTHOUGH TEACHING YOUR child good social skills goes a long way toward giving him the confidence he needs to deal with kids who tease and bully, you also want to provide some tips for handling tough situations.

- Let your child know he should tell you if someone is bothering him at school. Sometimes kids are afraid to let someone know they're being bullied for fear of retaliation. Also, they may feel ashamed and embarrassed.

- Reassure your child that you will work with her to improve the situation. It's not her fault, and it's not going to continue forever.
- Many experts suggest that ignoring a bully is one way to handle the situation. Bullies thrive on getting a reaction from their victims, so in theory, the less your child acts like the bully bothers him, the better off he'll be. Keep in mind, though, it's asking a lot of a child to ignore someone who's being blatantly rude, and some bullies may not stop their bad behavior even if they're ignored.
- Help your child project an image of confidence. Tell her that holding her head up high and making eye contact will make her look less appealing to a bully.
- Sometimes agreeing with the bully is all that's needed to defuse the situation. If your child is called "four-eyes" for wearing glasses, help him rehearse, saying something like, "Yeah, you're right. I wish my eyes were as perfect as yours, but they're not."
- Tell your child to look for opportunities to be nice to the bully. For example, approach her first and ask her what she did over the weekend.
- Encourage your child to hang out with his buddies. Kids are often bullied when they are by themselves. Bullies are less likely to approach a group of kids.
- Do not instruct your child to fight the bully. Fighting back not only satisfies the bully, it can also be dangerous.

If these tips don't help improve the situation, talk with school personnel and enlist their help. Often they're not aware of the situation. Once they know what's going on, they can observe more closely and intervene when necessary.

BECOMING SOCIALLY SAVVY: A LIFELONG
LEARNING PROCESS

IN THIS CHAPTER, we've given you a three-step plan for helping your child develop and improve his or her social skills. We've encouraged you not to overprotect your child, to teach your child persistence, and to show her how to focus on the right things. We've also given you tips on teaching your child to handle bullies and other "meanies." Developing social skills can be challenging for shy and anxious kids, but with your help and encouragement, they can learn the basics just like anyone else. Keep in mind that for all children—shy or outgoing—becoming socially savvy is a lifelong learning process. So take some pressure off yourself and your child. You've got plenty of time to practice, and we're confident your child will have some fun and make some friends in the process.

CHAPTER 9

Selective Mutism

When Your Child Is "Scared Speechless"

S HAWNDA BECAME concerned about her daughter, Mallory, when she was in preschool. She never said a single word to her teachers or the other children. One day she fell on the playground and cut her knee deeply, but she didn't tell the teacher what had happened. When someone noticed and directed her to the nurse's office, she became hysterical.

Later, when Shawnda came to pick up her daughter after learning what had happened, Mallory admitted she was afraid to talk to her teacher and she definitely didn't want to talk to the nurse. When Shawnda took her daughter to the pediatrician—both to check out her knee and to ask about her not speaking at school—the doctor said, "She's just shy. She'll grow out of it." Shawnda wasn't convinced, but she didn't know what else to do.

Mallory did not speak the entire year at her preschool, although she was quite talkative at home. Shawnda hoped that her daughter would start to talk at school in kindergarten—even just a few words—but it didn't happen. Fortunately, her kindergarten teacher recognized that Mallory had a problem, and they were referred to me for evaluation and treatment. I diagnosed Mallory with selective mutism.

WHAT IS SELECTIVE MUTISM?

SELECTIVE MUTISM IS a complex disorder characterized by an inability to speak in social situations. Children with selective mutism do not speak at school or in other public places where others might hear them, or they speak only in a barely audible whisper. These children speak freely and easily, however, at home with family members. This condition used to be called "elective mutism," reflecting the thinking that these children were deliberately not speaking, perhaps being stubborn or simply trying to get attention. Current theories argue that the problem is not elective. Rather, it's as if these children's voice boxes are frozen with fear, preventing them from communicating with words.

Recall that in Chapter 1 we said that mental health professionals use the *Diagnostic and Statistical Manual of Mental Disorders* to make diagnostic decisions. According to *DSM-IV*, a child has selective mutism if the following benchmarks are met:

- The child doesn't speak in certain select places, such as school or other social situations.
- The child can speak normally in at least one environment, usually the home.
- The child's inability to speak interferes with his or her ability to function normally in academic and/or social settings.
- The inability to speak has persisted for at least one month.
- The inability to speak is not caused by a communication disorder, such as stuttering, and does not occur as a part of other mental disorders, such as autism.

In the majority of cases, children with selective mutism also meet the criteria for social anxiety disorder. In addition to not being able to speak in certain situations, these children are typically shy, sensitive, and easily embarrassed. Along with this, there may be difficulty communicating nonverbally. For example, many children with selective mutism have difficulty making eye contact, look toward the ground, and sit or stand motionless, paralyzed by fear.

WHAT CAUSES SELECTIVE MUTISM?

FIRST, LET'S TALK about what does *not* cause selective mutism. There is no evidence that selective mutism is related to abuse, neglect, or trauma. This is important to state at the outset because, unfortunately, many families seeking help in the past have been wrongly accused of abuse. Studies have shown that children with selective mutism are no more likely to have experienced any type of abuse or trauma than are other children.

What does cause selective mutism, then? Many of the factors we discussed in Chapter 2 also hold true for the development of selective mutism. These children typically have a genetic predisposition to anxiety and are born with an inhibited temperament. Most of the families we've worked with report that they noticed differences in their child since infancy, such as sleep problems, frequent crying, and wariness in new situations. Once these children reach the age in which social interaction outside of the family is expected, parents often notice behaviors such as freezing, stiff posture, blank facial expressions, lack of smiling, as well as the inability to speak.

Learning can also contribute to the development and maintenance of selective mutism. These children experience extreme fear reactions when confronted with a situation where they are expected to speak—fear reactions no different from those of someone with a height phobia climbing onto the roof of a twenty-story building. Such reactions are intense and uncomfortable, often involving a number of physical symptoms. When the child successfully avoids the speaking encounter by withdrawing or freezing, the anxiety subsides. This reinforces the behavior and makes it more likely that the entire fear cycle will continue.

Keep in mind that by saying that learning factors are involved we are not saying these children are manipulating or doing this intentionally. This is not the case. Still, it's important to recognize the learning component to better guide treatment efforts.

In addition to genetic, biological, and learning factors, research indicates that a significant number of children with selective mutism have expressive language disorders, and a fairly large number come from bilingual environments. Although anxiety is still the underlying cause of the mutism, these factors no doubt play a role in certain cases.

A CLOSER LOOK

WHEN YOU LOOK more closely at children with selective mutism, you'll see that the inability to speak is just one—albeit an important—component of the problem. Frequently there are other associated characteristics:

- separation difficulties (unable to separate from parents or sleep alone)
- sensitivity to noise and touch (possible sensory integration difficulties)
- excessive worrying
- moodiness
- inflexibility

Children with selective mutism do have many positive characteristics. In general, they tend to be bright, creative, and perceptive. Their sensitivity makes them keenly aware of others' thoughts and feelings, and they can be very warm and loving. Although social relationships naturally tend to be difficult for them, they can be quite well liked by their peers. In fact, some peers may take on a protective role of the child with selective mutism, perhaps even talking for him or her.

In the vast majority of cases, children with selective mutism appear normal at home when they do not feel pressured to "perform."

They can be chatty, funny, happy-go-lucky, boisterous, and even bossy when they are comfortable and secure in their environment.

UNDIAGNOSED, MISDIAGNOSED, AND MISMANAGED

SELECTIVE MUTISM IS a heart-wrenching problem. Shawnda said that when she went to Mallory's school to help out on occasion, she didn't see the same little girl she saw at home. "Mallory never looked like she was having fun like the other kids were. I never saw her smile at school." Other parents have told us horror stories, such as their child not being able to eat a snack at school because he or she could not ask for it, or being punished for not talking. We hear of children being labeled as "oppositional" or "controlling." We've even heard of children not being able to advance a grade or go to a certain school because they were not able to take the necessary tests (for example, tests that included an oral component given by an unfamiliar examiner).

Then there are the letters we get through our Web site from families that are trying to get help for their child but who cannot find appropriate treatment. Some of these people, such as Shawnda, are told by a doctor that their child is "just shy" and "will grow out of it." Others are told their child may have autism or a learning disability. In most cases, professionals are well-meaning but simply grossly uninformed.

Sometimes, though, it's not the professionals holding up the process, but the parents. This can happen for a variety of reasons. First of all, remember that most children with selective mutism act perfectly normally at home. Even when teachers tell parents their child is not speaking at school, they may not recognize the severity of the problem.

In addition, because parents have likely been told by numerous people that their child is just shy, they may have difficulty considering another explanation. Because anxiety runs in families, it's also possible that one or both of the parents suffer with untreated social anxiety disorder, and therefore they may have trouble reaching out for help. Still other parents may worry about being suspected or accused of abuse. Finally, some parents may fear the ramifications of having their child labeled with a mental disorder.

All of these situations are understandable, but each delays the child in receiving the care he or she needs. Research shows that early diagnosis and treatment are vital. If you suspect that your child suffers from selective mutism, don't wait to seek help. The longer your child goes without speaking, the more difficult it is to break the pattern.

GETTING HELP: EVALUATION AND TREATMENT

THE FIRST STEP is to have your child see his or her pediatrician for a thorough physical exam to rule out any medical problem, and be sure to have your child's hearing checked. Assuming that your child's physical health checks out, the next step is to get a referral to a mental health professional. It may take some persistence, but try to find a therapist who is trained in anxiety disorders. Ask your doctor for a suggestion; talk to your child's school principal, guidance counselor, or nurse; review our resources section at the end of the book, or call your insurance company.

In a first session with a mental health professional, you'll be asked a lot of questions about your child's developmental, family, and medical history, as well as about behavioral characteristics your child may display. In addition, you'll probably be asked about any recent changes or stresses in the family. Your child may be present during this part of the evaluation, or you may be asked these background questions in a separate meeting.

The therapist will then spend some time getting to know your child. Don't worry. The therapist isn't expecting your child to talk. They may simply draw some pictures together or play a game of checkers. Occasionally the child talks with the therapist right off the bat. This does not automatically mean the child doesn't have selective mutism; it may be only in the school setting, for example, that the child cannot speak.

You may also want to request a speech and language evaluation, as 20–30 percent of children with selective mutism have subtle abnormalities in these areas. This is frequently done through the school system. Your therapist can help you decide if this is necessary.

Treatment of selective mutism is very similar to the methods for overcoming social anxiety we've already described and usually involves a combination of approaches, which we briefly describe below.

Gradual exposure. This method of exposure, which we described in Chapter 7, simply refers to the process of facing one's fears rather than avoiding them. This is done in a systematic, step-by-step manner in which the child confronts the least feared item first, gradually working his way up to more feared items. Exposures can be done either in real-life situations or in one's imagination.

Fading. Fading is another variant of the gradual exposure method. In this scenario, the exposure begins with a situation that is comfortable for your child, for example, talking with you in the hallway outside of the classroom with no one else around. Gradually, new variables are introduced to the situation, such as the teacher walking by and overhearing your child speak. Next, perhaps the teacher is at her desk working the entire time while you and your child are talking in the hallway.

Audio- and videotape techniques. Some families and therapists have successfully used audio- and videotape techniques to help in the exposure process. For example, your child reads into a tape recorder and then plays the recording for his teacher. This helps him become accustomed to having someone else hear him speak. Although not necessarily part of the treatment per se, it can help to videotape your child to show a new therapist or even a teacher how he interacts at home while in a comfortable situation.

Positive reinforcement. Of course, as we discussed in Chapter 3 and Chapter 4, many children benefit from a reward and incentive system to help motivate them to persevere through the difficult job of overcoming their fears.

Cognitive restructuring. Helping the selectively mute child change his or her thinking patterns must go hand in hand with the exposure methods. The goal is to help these kids revise their proba-bility distortions ("If I speak, other kids will notice and think I sound weird") as well as their severity distortions ("If other kids laugh at me, it will be the end of the world").

Family education.. Recall that we said that there is no evidence of increased family psychopathology in cases of selective mutism. Nonetheless, families need to be educated about what they can do to help in the treatment process. Families also benefit from support and from learning how to advocate for their child.

Relaxation techniques. Teaching a child with selective mutism relaxation techniques can help not only lower his overall anxiety level but also give him some coping skills he can use when progress-ing through the exposure therapy.

Medication. Medication is not always necessary, but it can some-times help the selectively mute child engage more fully in the ther-apy process. The guidelines we present in Appendix A, "Seeking Professional Help," will help you think through this issue. Keep in mind that medication should be used as a part of an overall treatment program. It is unlikely that medication alone will solve all the problems of a selectively mute child.

Let's return to Mallory's case to describe how these approaches work in a child with selective mutism.

BACK TO MALLORY

AS I EXPECTED, Mallory wasn't comfortable talking with me at first. But as we worked with puppets, she was able to make them move their heads to indicate yes or no responses to my questions. I like working with children, in part because their imaginations let me be creative when explaining basic concepts for relieving anxiety and reducing fear. For example, I taught Mallory some basic breathing techniques—children usually learn these quite easily—by having her imagine a balloon expanding and contracting in her belly. I taught her progressive muscle relaxation by having her pretend to squeeze a lemon in her hand and then release it, and so on. We drew pictures of ladders to show how she could overcome her fear of speaking by climbing the ladder, one rung at a time.

After some preliminary work of educating Mallory and her family about the process, we constructed a hierarchy of situations she was to complete. We also devised a reward system in which she would earn stickers for completing the items on her hierarchy. In addition, Mallory would get a stuffed bear she had been wanting after a specified amount of progress had been made. After Mallory worked her way through her initial hierarchy, we developed another one using more challenging tasks, such as asking aloud in class, "May I get a drink of water, please?"

Mallory's Hierarchy

1. Whisper aloud to Mom or Dad so that Jill (same-aged neighbor) can hear

2. Talk aloud to Jill with Mom or Dad present
3. Talk aloud to Jill without Mom or Dad present
4. Talk aloud to Mom or Dad in front of Jill's mother
5. Say one sentence to Jill's mother
6. Say a few words to an unfamiliar adult, such as a bank teller who gives her a piece of candy (for example, "Thank you")
7. Say hello to teacher at school with no other children present
8. Say hi to a classmate
9. Talk to teacher in presence of one other child
10. Talk to teacher in presence of several children

In addition to working with Mallory behaviorally on her hierarchy, I met with the family to teach them to stop reinforcing Mallory for not speaking. Mallory's siblings had become quite skilled at knowing what Mallory wanted or needed when they were in public and she wouldn't speak. This commonly happens when a child has selective mutism, and unless these dynamics are addressed, progress will be slowed.

Fortunately, Mallory's family was cooperative when they realized they weren't doing Mallory a favor by "helping" her in the ways they had been. Meanwhile, Mallory worked diligently to complete the items on the hierarchy. Of course, her parents were there to encourage her and keep her on the right track. Once the pattern was broken, though, it didn't take much time to see progress.

WHEN THE GOING GETS TOUGH: KAYLA'S STORY

UNFORTUNATELY, NOT ALL cases go as smoothly as Mallory's did. More typical is Kayla's story.

Kayla is a remarkably brave little girl who has worked hard to overcome selective mutism. I first became acquainted with her story when I was participating in a PBS documentary on social anxiety disorder called *Afraid of People*. The producer sent me an early rough cut of the documentary to watch, and I was particularly moved by

Kayla's story. Since then, I've corresponded regularly with Kayla's mother, Sherry, keeping abreast of Kayla's progress.

Kayla was shy and timid for as long as Sherry can remember. At family gatherings, Kayla stuck close by Sherry's side and had trouble interacting with the other kids—unless, however, the gathering was in their home, in which case she acted perfectly normally.

Sherry recalled one Halloween party when Kayla wouldn't participate in any of the activities. At the time, Sherry didn't know what was wrong and felt angry that Kayla was embarrassing her this way. "I feel horrible about it now," Sherry admitted, "but I yelled at Kayla the whole way home."

Preschool: Suffering in silence. Kayla started preschool when she was almost four years old. It was rough going from the beginning. Kayla wasn't able to initiate any type of play with the other children. It was as if she had become paralyzed with fear. Sherry thought it was just because she had never been in a school setting before and hoped that she'd adjust in time.

Unfortunately, Sherry learned from the preschool teacher that Kayla was not participating in any of the activities unless it was something that could be done directly from her seat. For example, after the children used their crayon boxes, they were to put them back on a shelf. Kayla was unable to do this. The teacher told Sherry it was as if they were having a power struggle to see who would put the crayon box back. She told Sherry that Kayla was just being "stubborn."

Another problem Kayla had that year was snacktime. After eating their snack, the children were to throw away their napkin. Again, Kayla was unable to leave her seat. The teacher's solution was to tell Kayla she couldn't have the snack unless she threw away her trash. Kayla literally couldn't do it, but the teacher again viewed her as being oppositional and defiant. Sherry said, "When I learned my poor child was sitting in a classroom with twenty-five other students and watching them eat a snack—all because she was afraid—I was angry."

Sherry switched schools the next year, hoping that Kayla would be treated better. Unfortunately, the situation was similar. Throughout this time period, Sherry talked with their family doctor, who told her Kayla was simply shy and would outgrow it. Sherry thought to herself, "Okay, maybe that's the case, but I've never seen anyone *so* shy."

Kindergarten: The frustration mounts. When Kayla started kindergarten, Sherry had high hopes. She thought Kayla's teacher was the best she could imagine—a former school counselor. Sherry did all she could to inform the teacher of Kayla's issues ahead of time, but it seemed to fall on deaf ears. Kayla suffered many questionable practices. For example, her teacher singled her out for not being able to say the Pledge of Allegiance and took her out to the hall, where Kayla was told firmly that she had "one more try at this."

Kayla developed major separation anxiety during this year. She started crying from the moment she woke up in the morning about having to go to school. Sherry would walk her into the classroom, then Kayla would chase Sherry out of the room when she left, crying hysterically. "I honestly didn't know what to do. I usually held it together at school but then cried all the way home," Sherry recalled.

All throughout her kindergarten year, Sherry received notes from Kayla's teacher telling her what a bad day Kayla had, how the children were frustrated with Kayla because she didn't talk, and how she saw only a "bleak future" for Kayla. "Talk about ripping a mother's heart out and stepping all over it," Sherry said.

Toward the end of Kayla's kindergarten year, Sherry first heard the term "selective mutism." She did all the research she could on the problem, talked again with her family doctor, and made an appointment for Kayla to see a psychiatrist.

The psychiatrist did, in fact, diagnose Kayla with selective mutism but didn't do much else to guide Sherry or her husband to help Kayla. He recommended medication, but because he did not explain his rationale, they didn't want to consider this option. Thinking back on it, Sherry believes that if the doctor had taken more time to explain the medication and what it was supposed to do, she would have been more open-minded.

First grade: Coming out of her shell. Kayla finally got an understanding, supportive teacher for first grade. This was the year she slowly began to thrive. She started out the year bonding with a boy who had cerebral palsy. Sherry described him as a loving little boy who always gave out hugs to kids. Kayla sat by him and his aide; because of his gentle ways, Kayla felt secure and accepted. "I think Kayla could look at him and his struggles with his speech and see that he didn't let it hold him back in life," Sherry said. Kayla began reading out loud to this boy, and she started talking to her teacher in a whisper.

Also during this time period, Sherry found a new physician, Dr. Elisa Shipon-Blum, D.O., an expert in selective mutism. Sherry said, "She was a dream come true for us. She had a complete understanding of anything and everything I said about my daughter. It was so good to have someone validate my feelings and concerns." Dr. Shipon-Blum educated Sherry and her husband about the benefits of medication, and they started Kayla on a very low dose of a serotonin selective reuptake inhibitor (SSRI). She also recommended cognitive-behavioral therapy for Kayla.

Positive changes in Kayla occurred almost immediately. She began to get out of the car at school with a little more confidence, and she even started waving to the crossing guard. "I will never forget the first time she yelled out the car window to one of her friends after school," Sherry said. "It was as if she finally discovered the voice she never knew she had." Kayla also began raising her hand in class and was able to ask to use the bathroom. One time, Kayla actually had to be told, along with her friends, to hold the noise down.

Sherry remembers that Kayla's fears started disappearing in other areas as well. "She started wanting to do things she'd never even tried before, like climbing trees and hanging upside down on her swing set." Sherry wondered if she had wanted to try these things for so long but never had the courage to do so.

Kayla blossoms. Kayla's school years keep getting better and better. During second grade, she began to speak out loud in small groups in the classroom. She has a wonderful group of friends who accept her for who she is. Most still see her struggle at school, mainly with speaking out in front of the class, but they just accept it. Sherry says, "She is actually liked so much the girls fight over who is going to play with her at recess." Compare this to kindergarten when the kids wouldn't play with Kayla.

Kayla can now talk with the majority of the adults in the school. She answers the teacher directly instead of talking through friends. She can speak on the telephone now, something she was previously unable to do. She is not afraid to try new things anymore; according to Sherry, she actually has a keen sense of adventure.

Sherry says that best of all, Kayla's self-confidence has grown: "She sees she can accomplish things in life."

Another brave person. Kayla is a brave little girl who's worked hard to overcome selective mutism. Kayla's not the only brave character in this story. Sherry played a remarkable role in making Kayla's story one of triumph. Throughout the process of finding help for Kayla, Sherry realized that she herself had probably suffered with social anxiety as a child and even into adulthood. Despite her own reticence, she became quite assertive in interacting with school and medical personnel who weren't always the easiest to deal with. She persisted and worked hard to put all the pieces of Kayla's situation together and to get Kayla the help she so desperately needed.

Just like Kayla, Sherry is growing in ways she never thought possible. She decided to go back to school and is working on her bachelor's degree in human services. She's active in the Selective Mutism–Childhood Anxiety Network and serves as a peer support person through their Web site. She is certainly a role model for us all.

REVIEW: SOME GUIDELINES

IF YOU SUSPECT that your child has selective mutism, here are some suggestions.

- Selective mutism is best treated early. If you child has not spoken in the classroom by midyear of kindergarten at the very latest, seek an evaluation from a mental health professional who is familiar with selective mutism.
- Reassure your child that you will be there through this tough time, offering plenty of support and encouragement.
- Do not force your child to speak or use any type of punishment to correct the problem. Instead, encourage your child gradually to meet small speaking-related goals.
- Recognize that there are many steps between not speaking and speaking. In the early stages, pointing, nodding, and using pictures to express needs can be encouraged.
- Not all cases go as smoothly as Mallory's did; some are more like Kayla's and take years to get the right diagnosis and treatment. Be patient, but keep at it!
- Some children may require medication as an adjunct to behavioral treatment. Don't be afraid to try medication if things are not going well using therapy alone.
- Read as much as you can about selective mutism. Check out the Selective Mutism Group on the Internet. There are tips for parents and teachers, support groups, an "Ask the Doctor" program, book listings and reviews, and two forums for those with selective mutism—teens and adults—to share thoughts and concerns. See the "Resources" section for the Web address.

|||||||||||||||||||||||||||||||||||||||||||||||||||||||||||||||||||||||||||||||||||

CHAPTER 10

School Anxiety

When Your Child Resists Going to School

J AVON AND Briana, a couple in their late thirties, came to see me because of problems they were having with their eleven-year-old daughter, Dominique. Dominique had always found transitions difficult. Whereas their other two children got into the swing of a new school year in a few weeks, it took Dominique many months before she felt even somewhat comfortable.

This was the first year of middle school, and things had gotten off to a rocky start. Dominique was extremely nervous about going to a new school, one that was much bigger and farther away. She had to take the bus, something she hadn't done before. On top of that, her best friend from grade school moved to another state over the summer. Dominique had always been painfully shy, and this was her only real friend. Dominique had seemed down in the dumps ever since her friend left.

Briana told me Dominique complained of abdominal pain nearly every day. She had taken her to the doctor, but nothing seemed medically wrong. By the second quarter of school, Dominique had been absent numerous times and her grades were lower than they'd ever been. Several of her teachers commented on her report card that she did not participate in class discussions and did not seem to be working up to her potential.

When Dominique did go to school, she made Briana drive her because she hated taking the bus. She said she was intimidated by the other kids and couldn't find a place to sit. Although this resulted in Briana being late to work, she went along with her daughter's requests because she appeared so visibly distraught. She didn't want to make Dominique feel worse than she already did.

One day, the school counselor caught Dominique skipping a class. When the counselor asked Dominique what was going on, she burst into tears and explained she was terrified of giving an oral book report due that day. The counselor called and asked the parents to come in for a conference. Javon, Briana, and the school counselor tried several interventions to help Dominique, but nothing seemed to work. The family was subsequently referred to me, but by this time, Dominique hadn't been to school for three consecutive weeks.

WHAT IS SCHOOL REFUSAL?

SCHOOL REFUSAL DESCRIBES children who either don't attend school or who have difficulty remaining in school. It is the term currently being used for what previously was called school phobia. Although children with school phobia usually exhibit fear and anxiety, it's not always the case that they're afraid of school itself, as the term implies. These children may have difficulty going to school or remaining in school for a variety of reasons. Dominique's concerns related to social anxiety. Other children may not want to attend school because they have a learning disability and school is difficult and frustrating for them. Still others might avoid going to school because they're tired and depressed and would rather stay in bed and sleep.

School refusal is not the same as truancy. Truant children are more typically defiant and deceptive, and their parents are not aware they are not in school. In contrast, school refusers more often than not are well behaved and compliant kids, except for this particular circumstance. In addition, their parents know they are not in school. These parents have likely spent plenty of time and energy trying to get their child to school, but with no success. In addition, school refusers make it to school but then have frequent somatic complaints, go to the nurse, and subsequently go home.

Although school refusal can occur for a variety of reasons, we've found that social anxiety is often a large component of the problem. School refusers tend to be shy, are often concerned about other people judging them, and take seriously what others say to them. These children usually have a strong need to please parents and teachers and try hard to obey all the rules.

The school setting can be extremely stressful for these kids. Many of them have fears of being bullied, they worry about classes such as physical education, and they are afraid of being criticized by teachers. It's important to make sure that any reality-based fears (if bullying is actually taking place) are addressed and promptly corrected.

In addition to social anxiety, separation anxiety is a common trigger for school refusal, and these two problems are often related. Frequently, separation anxiety is seen in younger children with school refusal. Keep in mind that some anxiety about starting school is normal for young children (we include tips on helping young children adjust below). Also note that not all kids who are school refusers have separation anxiety, and so for the purposes of simplicity we discuss separation anxiety in Chapter 11.

Back to School Time for Young Children: How Parents Can Help

1. Be enthusiastic about the upcoming change. If you are excited and confident, your child will be, too.
2. Prepare yourself. Take note of how your child reacts to separation. If possible, visit the new setting with your child. Introduce your child to the new teacher or early childhood professional in advance.

3. Arrange a playdate with another child from the program, preferably one-on-one, so that your child will see a familiar face when she walks in.
4. Start daily routines that will add to continuity. Let your child become involved with packing lunch or laying out clothes. Also, begin an earlier bedtime several weeks before.
5. Put aside extra time, particularly on the first day, for chatting and communicating together. But remember not to prolong the good-bye. If the child whines or clings, staying will only make it harder.
6. Always say good-bye to your child. Be firm, but friendly about separating. Never ridicule a child for crying. Instead, make supportive statements like, "It's hard to say good-bye."
7. At the end of the workday, put aside your concerns and focus on being a parent.

Back to School Time for Young Children: How Teachers Can Help

1. Make sure activities are developmentally appropriate for children. Interesting and challenging but doable activities will help children feel comfortable in their new setting.
2. Make an effort to get to know each individual child as quickly as possible. Parents can provide information about children's likes, dislikes, and special interests.
3. Welcome suggestions from families, particularly those of children with special needs. Parents can offer specific suggestions they have found useful for their own child, and advise on classroom setup and modifications.
4. Hold an orientation for children and parents. Small groups will make it easier for children to get to know one another.
5. Show children around the new school or program, introducing them to other adults who are there to help them become acclimated.

6. Create partnerships between preschools and elementary schools in the community. Meetings may focus on the sharing of ideas and concerns.

7. Set up an area for photos of parents and family members that children may "visit" throughout the day. Also include items that reflect the cultural experience of all children to help promote a sense of mutual respect and understanding. Children, just like adults, need time to adjust to new people and situations. Experience can make transition a bit easier, but even with experience, change can be stressful. Patience and understanding on the part of parents and teachers or caregivers will help children learn how to approach new situations with confidence—a skill that will help them make successful transitions all through life.

THROUGH THE YEARS: COMMON CONCERNS KIDS HAVE ABOUT SCHOOL

BEFORE WE DISCUSS what to do about school refusal, we present some common concerns kids may experience at different stages of their academic life. For example, we already noted that separation anxiety triggers school anxiety for many preschoolers. In contrast, dressing out for physical education classes commonly worries socially anxious kids in middle school. The lists below are certainly not all-inclusive, but they will give you an idea of the range of concerns kids can experience at different ages.

Preschool

- Being away from home, possibly for the first time—"I'll miss my mommy too much."
- A new place; a new teacher—"Will I know where to go? Will I remember my teacher's name?"

- All new children to get to know—"Who will play with me?"
- Being in a structured setting, possibly for the first time—"What are the rules? What if I forget what I'm supposed to do?"

Elementary School

- New and unfamiliar teachers.
- Possibly less intimate environment than preschool.
- A bigger school building may be intimidating.
- Finding the bathroom, the cafeteria, and so on.
- May have to ride the bus for the first time.
- Increased pressure to be popular, especially in later grades.
- Friends may be separated into different classrooms.
- May be overwhelmed by the increased stimulation.
- May come home tired and cranky after "holding it together" all day at school.
- Especially during the later elementary years, shyness and anxiety begin to be noticed by peers and in our culture are not generally valued.

Middle School

- A new and larger school, perhaps farther away.
- Children from many different elementary schools getting grouped into one middle school—lots of unfamiliar faces.
- Changing classrooms and teachers for every subject.
- Little time between classes; hallways and bathrooms may be crowded.
- Dealing with lockers.
- May have to dress out for physical education class.
- Increase in teasing and bullying.
- Dealing with lunch—no more assigned seating and less adult supervision.
- More social expectations—extracurricular activities, school dances, and so on.
- An increase in cliques.

Adolescence

- Rapid physical and hormonal growth can lead to greater awkwardness and self-consciousness.
- Emotions tend to fluctuate, sometimes extremely.
- More complex social relationships; pressure to date.
- Pressure to conform; experimentation with alcohol and drugs.
- Increased academic pressures.
- Possibly dealing with part-time jobs.
- Identity issues: Who am I?

Now that you have an idea of what some of your child's concerns may be, let's look at what to do if your child is reluctant, or even refusing, to go to school.

HOW BEST TO HANDLE SCHOOL REFUSAL

THERE ARE A number of things to keep in mind when handling school refusal.

If your child is complaining of physical symptoms, have her checked by a physician. This is an important first step. It's unlikely that anything is physically wrong with your child, but you don't want to make that assumption and later find you were wrong. Do this as soon as you realize there's a problem. The sooner you're able to begin treating the school refusal from a cognitive-behavioral perspective, the easier the treatment will be on everyone involved.

Look for patterns of when your child complains of illness. Does he wake up with a stomachache or headache? Does he complain of these things when he's busy and distracted? Does he feel ill on Saturdays? Be objective and play detective. Do this in a low-key, nonaccusatory way; there's no point in putting your child on the defensive. Look for clues as to what is causing your child to avoid school. One family we worked with had such sporadic problems with their child it was hard to see a pattern. The boy wasn't very adept at articulating his concerns, which made putting the pieces of the puzzle together more difficult. Finally, the father noticed that it was on days when their son had band that he developed the stomachaches. They found out there was a boy picking on him in band class and their son was too shy to tell the teacher. "I didn't want the teacher to be mad and say I was tattling," their son later told them.

Set up a conference with the teacher and the school counselor. We recommend that both parents attend the conference for several reasons. First, it sends the message to the school that you're both involved and both committed to working on the problem. And second, too often it's the mothers who bear the brunt of the problems with children who refuse to go to school. It can be extremely stressful and challenging dealing with such a problem. Having both parents involved helps stack the deck in favor of success.

Approach the conference with an open mind. Don't assume the teacher or the school has done something wrong. Similarly, teachers should not assume the problem lies with the parents. When stress levels are high, it's natural to want to point the finger and blame someone, but it doesn't do much to solve the problem. Try to have an open discussion about what might be going on. If there are situations at school, such as bullying, that cause concern, this is the time to discuss them. Remember that the school is more likely to hear you out if you stay calm and make your points in a nonaccusatory manner. Most teachers and schools are doing the best they can with often limited resources. Teachers and school personnel should also remember that it's not always the parents' fault, and the vast majority of parents have their children's best interests at heart.

Talk with your child about what's bothering her, while at the same time making it clear that a plan will be made to return to school. Remember what we've said about there being many possible causes for school refusal. Don't assume that you know what the problem is. Talk with your child about what is bothering her, while at the same time conveying the fact that she will, in fact, go to school. Keep in mind, though, that some children can't describe what is bothering them. Don't force conversation if it doesn't seem to be going anywhere.

On the other hand, avoid lengthy discussions and debates about the importance of going to school. Don't lecture. It won't do any good, and it may actually make matters worse. Any attention, even negative attention, can reinforce and maintain a problem. However, as we've stated before, address any legitimate concerns as soon as possible.

The most important message to convey is this: You believe your child can conquer this problem, and you'll be there to help her through it.

Do not make it appealing to stay at home. Let your child know that if he's truly ill, he will need to see a doctor, stay in bed and rest, keep the TV off, and so on. Enforce rules about no TV or video games. This may sound obvious, but I'm amazed at how many kids stay home and basically have free rein of the house, doing whatever they please. Also, if your child complains of being ill and says he needs to stay home, let him know you will be calling the doctor's office for an appointment. Children often won't want to see the doctor, so this may serve as a deterrent for some. If you stay home with your child, don't offer lots of extra attention and sympathy. It may sound cruel, but you don't want staying at home to be appealing.

If it's clear your child is not sick, but for whatever reason he is not in school, simulate a learning environment as much as possible. Have him read, study, sit upright at a desk, and so forth. For adolescents, you may also want to make sleeping off-limits, as this is alluring for many in this age group. Some of these suggestions will prove difficult to follow for working parents, but do your best. Consider enlisting the aid of a nonworking friend, relative, or neighbor for a short period of time.

Make it a policy that unless your child has a fever, she needs to go to school. If your child frequently complains of some physical problem in the morning before school, make it a rule that unless she has a fever, she goes to school. If the child is truly ill, the school nurse can evaluate the situation and send her home if necessary. In the chaos of the morning—trying to get everyone ready for school and work—this removes the power struggle from the parent and child, which is a good thing. Too often, the struggle itself can be reinforcing for children because they are receiving so much extra attention. Along the same lines, don't spend much time, if any, discussing physical symptoms, especially if a doctor has already determined there is nothing medically wrong.

Consider having someone else take your child to school until the situation is resolved. Because emotions are so charged during a time like this, it can be helpful to remove yourself from the job of having to force your child to go to school. If there is related separation anxiety with the mother, having the father take the child to school can often help. Or have a friend or another family member be in charge of these transition times until the child has made a successful reentry into school.

Many people do not realize how draining it can be trying to get these children to school. I witnessed the drama firsthand with Monica, who was in the third grade and had been out of school for about a month. There seemed to be no clear-cut trigger for the change in her behavior. Prior to this time she had reliably made it to school each day. She had a short stretch of separation anxiety in kindergarten, although it was apparently nothing like this.

I saw Monica and her family for several sessions, and we made a plan to return her to school. The day came when her parents were to take her to school directly after an appointment at my office. Monica said all the right things. She stated that she knew she had to return to school and that she was ready.

As I walked the family out to the checkout window, I had a gut-feeling that things had gone almost too smoothly. Something didn't feel quite right, although I couldn't put my finger on it exactly. While the parents were paying the co-pay and making a follow-up appointment, the secretary told me that my next patient had canceled. I decided to take heed of my intuition and asked the parents if they'd mind if I rode along to school with them.

As I sat in the backseat with Monica, her protests began: We were all mean for making her go to school, she hated us, and she wasn't going. That was that! I used my best empathic listening skills and validated Monica's feelings while calmly stating—like a broken record—that she would, indeed, be going to school that day.

Trying to get Monica out of the car was like trying to get a scared dog into the vet's office. Somehow we managed to get her out, but when we got to the entrance of the school, she spread her arms and legs so as not to fit through the door. Meanwhile, she was screaming at the top of her lungs.

I got a glimpse of how embarrassing these situations must be for parents. Here I was, the psychologist, having a heck of a time getting this child into her classroom.

What's interesting to note is that when we did get her to class, she made it through the whole day without incident, and she went to school each day thereafter without a fight. She told me later that she didn't want to risk having her therapist "pull another stunt like that."

The longer your child remains home, the harder it will be to return to school. In most cases, consider "homebound" schooling only as a last resort; at the very least, make sure your child knows from the start that this is a time-limited arrangement. School refusal is the kind of problem that you must act on quickly. As soon as you suspect there's a problem, follow the suggestions in this chapter and seek help if you don't get results quickly on your own. The longer children stay home, the harder it is for them to return. Many of these children especially worry about what the other kids will say about their absence. You may want to rehearse something for your child to say and even role-play it together. Also, certain times seem easier to return to school than others. Returning on a Monday is easier than a Friday; similarly, returning after a break is sometimes desirable. It seems less notice is paid to the returning child in such a scenario.

SEEK SUPPORT FOR YOURSELF

ALTHOUGH IT'S UNSETTLING to see your child intensely distressed about attending school, it's imperative that you remain calm and supportive but ultimately firm. Rally whatever support you need: Enlist the aid of a friend or neighbor, the school counselor, or a therapist. If your child has really dug in his heels, you may need the strength of numbers on your side. This isn't the time to cave in. Your child *needs* to go to school—this is where children mature, not only intellectually but also socially and emotionally. By following the above suggestions, there's every reason to believe that your child will overcome his school anxiety and, in the process, gain a newfound appreciation of his ability to hang in there and work through a tough situation.

CHAPTER 11

Alphabet Soup: GAD, SAD, OCD, PTSD, and More

When Your Child Suffers from Other Problems

I F YOUR child suffers from more than social anxiety disorder, you're not alone. Having an additional psychiatric diagnosis is more the rule rather than the exception. Oftentimes anxiety disorders coexist—for example, a child may have social anxiety disorder and generalized anxiety disorder—and, frequently, depression accompanies the anxiety. Because many of the symptoms of anxiety and depression overlap, it can be complicated to tease apart the different diagnoses.

Fortunately, the treatment methods we've described in this book go a long way toward helping kids overcome a variety of anxiety problems, as well as depression. Still, it can be helpful to know just what you're dealing with. In this chapter, we share stories of children who have social anxiety in combination with either another anxiety disorder or depression. For the purposes of this chapter, we focus less on the social anxiety and more on the coexisting disorder.

After each story and description of the disorder, we've included some screening questions (taken from the *DSM-IV*) for you to ask yourself about your child. Keep in mind that answering these questions is not a substitute for a clinical diagnostic interview from a psychologist or other trained mental health professional. Nonetheless, the information you gain will help you better know the direction you need to go. We also offer some tips on dealing with more than one disorder.

WHEN YOUR CHILD WORRIES TO DEATH

BRANDON, A JUNIOR in high school, had final exams in three and a half weeks. He told himself he had to get straight A's or he'd never get into a good college. He worried so much he couldn't fall asleep at night. The next day he was too tired to concentrate at school, much less study when he got home in the afternoon. His stomach hurt all the time, he lost his appetite, and he came down with a bad cold.

Brandon's worries encompassed more than getting good grades. He also worried that his father might lose his job. True, his father worked for the state of Missouri and there had been a lot of layoffs; however, his father's department hadn't been touched by the budget crunch, and there was no reason to expect that he would lose his job. Even if he did, Brandon's mother worked and made a good income.

Brandon also worried about his little sister's health. She had asthma and came down with frequent upper respiratory problems; still, his worry was out of proportion to the situation—his parents were taking good care of her.

Brandon's parents described him as a good kid—bright, kind, sensitive, and caring. Unfortunately, Brandon wasn't leading the life of a normal teenager. He was too busy worrying. Sure, teenagers have their ups and downs and their worries, but Brandon's anxiety was over the top, and he suffered from what's called generalized anxiety disorder, or GAD.

What is GAD? The key feature of generalized anxiety disorder is excessive and seemingly uncontrollable worry. Kids with GAD are often described as worrywarts. They exhibit concerns in a number of areas, such as grades, friends, sports, health, safety, general conditions in the world, and so on. The worry is next to impossible for these kids to "turn off." Along with the worry, these children may have physical complaints including stomachaches, headaches, and muscle tension. Frequently, kids with GAD ask for a lot of reassurance from their parents or teachers, but the reassurance does little to ease their troubled minds.

Does Your Child Have Generalized Anxiety Disorder?

1. Has your child worried more days than not for at least six months about a number of events or activities?
2. Does your child have trouble turning off the worry?
3. Does the worry cause your child a great deal of distress? Does it affect his or her functioning at school or at home?
4. Has your child experienced any of the following symptoms, with at least some of the symptoms being present on most days?
   - restlessness or feeling keyed up or on edge
   - easily fatigued, tired
   - difficulty concentrating
   - irritability
   - muscle tension
   - difficulty falling asleep or staying asleep
   - headaches or stomachaches

If you answered yes to questions 1, 2, and 3, and your child has at least three of the physical symptoms listed under 4, your child may have generalized anxiety disorder.

WHEN YOUR CHILD WON'T LEAVE YOUR SIDE

LAURIE IS A BRIGHT and capable ten-year-old girl. She's always been on the shy side. She's slow to make friends, doesn't participate in class, and is sensitive to criticism. "I've never had to punish Laurie," said her mother, Susan. "She usually does what she's told, and if she doesn't, all I have to do is give her a stern look and she gets right to it. If I ever raise my voice, she breaks into tears." Laurie likely has social anxiety disorder, but this isn't what initially brought them to see me.

"I'm at my wit's end," Susan told me. "I've missed so much work because of Laurie's problem, I'm on the verge of losing my job." Laurie's father had taken off work and joined us for the initial session; his life wasn't quite as disrupted as Susan's, but he was concerned as well.

For the past two months, Laurie had experienced an increasing amount of difficulty separating from Susan. It began with not wanting to go to school. She threw a fit about taking the school bus and insisted that Susan drive her. She couldn't say what specifically bothered her about the bus, but Susan had given in because Laurie seemed truly distressed.

Then Laurie started going to the school nurse's office regularly with stomachaches. Laurie would beg to call her mother at work. The nurse always tried to delay Laurie calling her mother, but the intensity of her crying usually resulted in the nurse allowing it. Some days, Laurie would throw such a fit that the nurse would tell Susan she needed to pick Laurie up and take her home.

Of course, Susan had taken Laurie to the pediatrician after this had gone on for a few weeks. A thorough physical exam and some tests indicated that there was no medical problem. Although the doctor thought it was "just stress," he prescribed an antacid to help calm Laurie's stomach.

Susan hoped the medicine would help the situation. Unfortunately, things went from bad to worse. Laurie started having trouble falling asleep at night. She insisted that her mother lie with her until she fell asleep. She also started having nightmares that something horrible was going to happen to her mother. She worried that her mother might die in a car accident or be diagnosed with cancer.

Soon her fears generalized to bad weather. If the sky was the slightest bit gray, she worried there would be a storm and that something would happen to her mother. Susan couldn't go to the supermarket anymore without Laurie having an emotional meltdown. Even being on different floors of their home was a problem for Laurie, and she followed Susan everywhere.

Laurie felt embarrassed and ashamed about her behavior, but she felt she had no control over it. "I can't help myself from having these fits," she told me.

Laurie's official diagnosis was separation anxiety disorder, and as we mentioned previously, she likely suffers from social anxiety disorder as well.

What is separation anxiety disorder? Many children experience separation fears when they're away from a parent or a familiar place; however, normal separation fears are typically outgrown by the age of five or six. Separation anxiety disorder affects between 2 to 3 percent of grade-school children and involves undue distress over day-to-day separation from parents or home. As we saw with Laurie, these children also have unrealistic fears of harm befalling loved ones. They may also "shadow" their parents, not letting them out of their sight. Separation anxiety disorder typically begins between the ages of seven and eleven, and it can occur abruptly in some situations.

Does Your Child Have Separation Anxiety Disorder?

1. Does your child display inappropriate and excessive anxiety concerning separating from home or from parents (or other people he or she is very close to)?

2. Does your child worry excessively about losing a parent or about possible harm coming to him or her?
3. Does your child worry about getting lost or getting kidnapped?
4. Is your child reluctant or unwilling to go to school or other places because of a fear of separation?
5. Does your child have an excessive fear of being alone?
6. Does your child have difficulty going to sleep without being near a parent or other close person?
7. Does your child experience repeated nightmares involving themes of separation?
8. Has this anxiety persisted for at least one month?
9. Is the anxiety causing significant distress or disturbances in academic, social, or other important areas of functioning?

If you answered yes to at least three of questions 1–7, and yes to 8 and 9, your child may have separation anxiety disorder.

WHEN YOUR CHILD DOES THINGS OVER AND OVER AGAIN

JUSTIN'S PARENTS KNEW he had social anxiety disorder. He'd previously seen a therapist and had progressed well with making friends and generally becoming more comfortable in a variety of social situations. When Justin turned ten, however, he developed a new set of anxieties.

One day, when they were getting ready to go to school, Justin's mom noticed he was taking a very long time coming down the stairs. She urged him to hurry, but he kept tapping the banister and counting out loud. At first she thought he was playing around, and she got angry. "Hurry up, Justin! We're late for school," she exclaimed. She shrugged it off, but when it happened again the next morning, she thought it was odd.

During this same time period, Justin began complaining about a girl at school. He said she looked "dirty" and that he was afraid he would get lice from sitting near her. He went to great lengths to avoid sitting by her. He even started making a ruckus in class one day—he knew he would get moved to a special "safe seat" where kids went when they needed to settle down. The teacher noticed that he also spent a great deal of time in the bathroom, and Justin's mother noticed that his hands were chapped and red. Justin had apparently been washing his hands over and over again when he thought he had come into contact with something this girl had touched.

Justin's parents took him back to the psychologist who had previously worked with them on his social anxiety, and he was subsequently diagnosed with obsessive-compulsive disorder (OCD).

What is OCD? Affecting approximately 1 to 3 percent of school-aged children, OCD is an anxiety disorder characterized by intrusive thoughts of something bad happening (for example, "I will be contaminated") and behaviors that are designed to ward off the bad thing from occurring (washing hands over and over). Kids with OCD often describe their obsessions as "worries," which can make it difficult to distinguish from GAD. The distinguishing feature is that the child with OCD must perform a ritual to counteract the obsession.

Common obsessions include fears of germs, contamination, or some type of harm or danger. For example, a child may fear that his house will catch on fire and have to repeatedly check to make sure small appliances are unplugged. Similarly, a child may fear that her house will be burglarized and have to check over and over again to see if doors are locked.

Other children may have obsessions related to "bad words" or "blasphemous" thoughts. For example, one child was afraid to take her first Communion because she had intrusive thoughts, such as, "What if I'm not really a Christian?" and "Jesus isn't God." This went beyond normal questioning, as she also had obsessive thoughts such as "Jesus sucks." This child's compulsions revolved around having to touch the Bible a certain number of times and saying, "Father forgive me."

Children with OCD often go undiagnosed for a long period of time because they are so embarrassed and deeply ashamed that they'd rather hide the problem than seek help.

Does Your Child Have OCD?

1. Does your child experience obsessions, as defined below?
   - Recurrent and persistent thoughts, impulses, or images that are experienced as intrusive and inappropriate and cause a great deal of distress.
   - The thoughts are not simply excessive worries about real-life problems.
   - The thoughts are extremely difficult to ignore or suppress.
2. Does your child experience compulsions, as defined below?
   - Repetitive behaviors, such as handwashing or checking, that he or she feels driven to do in response to the obsession.
   - The compulsions are aimed to reduce distress or prevent some dreaded event from happening, and are clearly excessive.
3. Does your child spend a significant amount of time dealing with his or her obsessions and compulsions (more than one hour per day)? Or do the obsessions and compulsions interfere with day-to-day functioning and relationships?

If you answered yes to all of the questions, your child may have obsessive-compulsive disorder.

WHEN YOUR CHILD CAN'T GET OVER SOMETHING

FIVE-YEAR-OLD ALICE sat in the backseat of a van, along with her little sister. Her mother had just picked them up from the babysitter's house. Her mother was cautious as they pulled out from the gravel driveway onto the country road—people often drove too fast along that stretch. With the sun setting and hitting the windshield just so, she missed seeing an oncoming vehicle whizzing by, and there was a horrible collision. Although she and the children suffered only minor injuries, the other driver was thrown from her car. Emergency vehicles arrived on the scene, and they learned the woman had lost her unborn child.

Alice was traumatized by the accident. For months she refused to ride in the van if her mother was driving. She would ride with her father if she absolutely had to, although she usually had a tantrum ahead of time. Although her younger sister didn't seem as affected, the two of them played every day with their dolls and acted out the accident. Alice would also put a pillow in her shirt and pretend she was pregnant. Then she would take the pillow out and say, "My baby died." Alice also developed nightmares, became very clingy, and cried more than usual.

Alice's parents understood that she was having a hard time dealing with the accident, and they tried to be understanding. They rightly grew concerned, however, when she seemed unable to get over it. The accident happened nearly six months ago, and Alice still didn't seem to be herself.

What is post traumatic stress disorder (PTSD)? As the name implies, PTSD can occur after someone is exposed to a traumatic experience. The experience might be a motor vehicle accident, as was the case with Alice, or it could be another situation in which the child felt threatened in some way. A natural disaster such as a tornado may trigger PTSD in some children, as may a burglary or some other type of crime. Physical or sexual abuse may also lead to PTSD in children.

Symptoms of PTSD include reexperiencing the trauma in some way, frequently in the form of nightmares or disturbing recollections of the event. Some children also develop difficulty sleeping and become extremely irritable or edgy. Another cardinal symptom of

PTSD is avoidance. The child seeks to avoid things associated with the trauma. For example, Alice didn't want to ride in a vehicle with her mother after the accident.

Does Your Child Have PTSD?

1. Has your child been exposed to a traumatic event in which both of the following statements are true?
   - He or she experienced or witnessed an event that involved actual or threatened death or serious injury, to either himself or herself or to others.
   - Your child's response was one of fear, helplessness, or horror.
2. Is your child "reexperiencing" the traumatic event in one or more of the following ways?
   - Recurrent and intrusive recollections of the event, which may include thoughts or images
   - Recurrent and distressing dreams about the event
   - Feelings as if the event is recurring—flashbacks
   - Intense distress when confronted with reminders of the event
3. Is your child avoiding things associated with the traumatic event?
   - Efforts to avoid thoughts or feelings associated with the trauma
   - Efforts to avoid people, activities, and places associated with the trauma
   - Inability to remember certain aspects of the trauma
4. Does your child feel jumpy or irritable? Is he or she having trouble sleeping? Difficulty concentrating?

If you answered yes to all of the above questions, and if the symptoms have lasted a month or more following the trauma and are adversely affecting your child's functioning, your child may have PTSD.

WHEN YOUR CHILD EXPERIENCES ANXIETY
ATTACKS "OUT OF THE BLUE"

JANE, IN THE eighth grade, complained off and on throughout the first semester of feeling "weird." She told her mother that her "heart beats funny" and that she got dizzy in the hallways. Her mother took her to the pediatrician, but the doctor didn't find anything medically wrong. Jane wasn't convinced, though.

One day while walking to her locker, Jane's heart began racing, she felt dizzy, and she was hot and sweaty. She knew she was probably too young, but the first thing that crossed her mind was that she was having a heart attack. A friend helped her get to the nurse's office and Jane's mother came to pick her up from school.

Jane stayed home from school for a few days. Her mother thought maybe she had a virus that was causing her not to feel well. Jane lay on the couch and cried off and on, worrying about her health. She talked incessantly to her parents about what could be wrong with her.

When Jane returned to school, these "attacks" began to happen more frequently. Once she was sitting at her desk reading and she started to feel "weird." She thought to herself, "Oh, my God. Here it comes again."

After a few more visits to the pediatrician, Jane was referred to a pediatric cardiologist. Still nothing medical was found, and she was referred to me.

What is panic disorder? Jane was on her way to developing panic disorder. Although it's rare in children, adolescents may develop the problem. To define panic disorder, we must first define a panic attack. A panic attack is a sudden rush of fear or discomfort accompanied by a number of physical symptoms such as shortness of breath, rapid heart rate, dizziness, sweating, tingling sensations in the extremities, trembling, choking sensations, chills or hot flashes, and nausea. In addition, feelings of unreality, fear of losing control, or fear of dying may accompany the physical symptoms.

Panic attacks can occur in the context of any of the anxiety disorders. For example, a child with social anxiety disorder may have a panic attack just before he has to stand in front of the class and give an oral report. A child with OCD may have a panic attack if she believes she's been in contact with something that is "contaminated." A child with GAD may have a panic attack while worrying. The defining feature of panic disorder is that the panic attacks are seemingly not triggered by anything—they come "out of the blue."

Does Your Child Have Panic Disorder?

1. Does your child experience recurrent, unexpected panic attacks? By unexpected, we mean they seem to come out of the blue.

2. Has at least one of these attacks been followed by at least a monthlong period of concern about having another panic attack?

   and/or

   Has your child worried a great deal about the consequences of a panic attack? ("Is something physically wrong?" or "Am I going crazy?")

   and/or

   Has your child's behavior changed since having the panic attack?

If you answered yes to question 1 and yes to at least one of the questions under 2, your child may have panic disorder.

WHEN YOUR CHILD IS DOWN IN THE DUMPS

ZACK, AGE THIRTEEN, attended a Catholic school. He was at the age where the boys began participating in the church services, both during the school week and on Sundays. Zack couldn't imagine being an altar boy. He could barely raise his hand in class to answer a question—how would he ever be able to walk around in front of the entire congregation? He was petrified he'd make a mistake and embarrass himself.

Zack's parents were disappointed, but they didn't push him. They knew he was extremely shy and had a difficult time performing in front of other people. Despite being musically inclined, he had already dropped out of choir and orchestra due to his performance anxiety.

The other kids gave Zack a hard time about not being an altar boy. Zack didn't want to be an altar boy, but he also hated standing out by not being one. He didn't know how to respond when kids asked him why he wasn't participating like all the other boys. He usually fell silent, staring at the ground.

"I feel like such a loser," he told his parents. "All the kids think I'm strange."

Zack started withdrawing more and more. His parents knew he was pretty quiet at school, but he was usually friendly and cheerful at home. Now he didn't talk much at home, either, and he didn't watch TV or play games with the family. Zack also was eating less, and he seemed to have less energy than usual.

Zack's situation is common. Kids who suffer from social anxiety disorder frequently wind up getting depressed as well. Consider the fact that all day long, every day, they face social and performance situations in which they feel they don't measure up. This takes a toll on their self-esteem and can easily spiral into a clinical depression.

What does depression in children look like? Depression in children looks a lot like depression in adults, although there can be differences. Kids with depression may look sad and sullen, or they may be more crabby and irritable than usual. They may lose interest in activities they once found enjoyable.

Loss of appetite and difficulty sleeping are also common symptoms of depression in children. Adolescents, on the other hand, may eat and sleep too much. It can go in either direction.

Problems concentrating can also go hand in hand with depression. For this reason, their grades in school may go down.

Depressed children may make self-deprecating comments, such as, "I'm no good" or "I hate myself." They may even get so down that they contemplate suicide.

Warning Signs of Possible Suicide

- talking directly or indirectly about committing suicide or wanting to die
- depression, sadness
- change in eating or sleeping habits
- boredom, withdrawal, and loss of interest in activities
- mood shifts
- giving away prized possessions
- an increase in alcohol or drug use
- a decrease in school performance
- a recent experience of loss
- a previous suicide attempt

Is Your Child Depressed?

Consider the previous two weeks when answering these questions.

1. Has your child acted down in the dumps, sad, or irritable nearly every day?
2. Has your child lost interest or pleasure in almost all of the activities he or she used to enjoy?
3. Has your child's appetite changed? Has his or her weight fluctuated?
4. Is your child having difficulty falling asleep? Staying asleep? Is your adolescent sleeping all the time?
5. Does your child seem uptight, restless, or edgy?

6. Does your child seem to have low energy and feel tired nearly every day?
7. Is he or she expressing feelings of worthlessness (for example, "I'm no good" or "People would be better off without me")?
8. Is he or she having difficulty concentrating?
9. Has your child made any statements about death or wanting to commit suicide?

If you answered yes to questions 1 and 2, and you to four or more additional questions, and these symptoms have been occurring together for two weeks, your child may be experiencing a clinical depression.

OTHER PROBLEMS YOU MAY SEE

ALTHOUGH OTHER ANXIETY disorders and depression are probably the most common problems that coexist with social anxiety disorder in children, there are some other conditions you'll want to be aware of. We describe them briefly below. Keep in mind that this is not an all-inclusive list. If your child has problems we don't mention, be sure and talk with your doctor and seek a referral to a mental health professional for further evaluation.

Substance abuse. Individuals with social anxiety disorder are particularly susceptible to developing problems with substance abuse. Alcohol (and sometimes recreational drugs) is often readily available at social events, and it doesn't take anxious people long to start believing that drinking helps them calm down and perhaps even makes them more outgoing. Adolescents, who are naturally prone to doing what "all the other kids are doing," frequently experiment with drugs and alcohol. When shy kids use these substances as a way to cope with their fear and anxiety, they're likely to end up with two problems instead of one.

The good news is that as your shy and anxious teen overcomes her fears, she probably won't have the same motivation to drink or use drugs. Of course, the substance abuse may have become a habit with a life of its own, and for this reason you need to deal with both problems.

If you suspect your son or daughter has a problem with substance abuse in addition to social anxiety disorder, here are some suggestions and things to think about:

- Don't take a wait-and-see approach. Talk with your teen right away about your concerns.
- It can be dangerous to drink while taking many prescription medications for depression and anxiety. Make sure your teen knows this and follows the guidelines for the particular medication.
- Talk with your teen about the fact that despite the immediate perception that alcohol has a calming effect, it actually increases anxiety over the long term.
- Studies show that people drinking a placebo (something they thought was an alcoholic beverage) did just as well socially as those drinking alcohol. Furthermore, even the placebo decreased inhibitions, leaving these people feeling more relaxed and outgoing.
- There is an Alcoholics Anonymous group just for teens called Alateen. We know going to group meetings can be overwhelming for those with social anxiety, but if your teen can muster the courage, it is worth a try. Reassure your son or daughter that there will be others there with social anxiety.

Sensory integration dysfunction. Does your child refuse to wear certain clothing or touch certain types of materials? Does the grass feel funny on his toes? Is he a picky eater? Is he overreactive to sights ("The sun is too bright") and sounds ("That noise hurts my ears")? Does your child avoid active games and activities, preferring instead to remain in one spot? Does your child tire easily? Does she seem awkward, uncoordinated, or accident-prone?

These are all telltale signs of sensory integration dysfunction, a common but frequently missed problem in which messages from the senses aren't correctly processed by the brain. SI dysfunction was first identified decades ago by an occupational therapist, but it has only recently received attention from doctors and psychologists.

Because children with social anxiety disorder are frequently overly sensitive (recall the discussion of behavioral inhibition in Chapter 2), it makes sense that a certain percentage of them also have problems with sensory integration. If the above descriptions sound like your child, consider requesting an occupational therapy (OT) evaluation. This is the type of professional best trained to evaluate sensory concerns. Most school districts have an occupational therapist on staff who could at least do a basic screening. Also, the best resource we've found on sensory integration is *The Out-of-Sync Child* by Carol Stock Kranowitz (see Resources).

Attention deficit disorder (ADD) and attention deficit hyperactivity disorder (ADHD). The key features of ADD and ADHD are inattention, distractibility, impulsivity. These children have difficulty focusing and paying attention, and they often have difficulty in school as a result. Kids with ADHD also display high levels of motor activity. In other words, they appear to be always on the go. In contrast, kids with ADD (and not the hyperactivity part) are often described as "spacey."

Because children with both ADD and ADHD can have difficulty processing incoming information, they often have social problems. They may not "read" social cues correctly and can unknowingly annoy other people. Often these kids are then left out of group activities and may become isolated. In addition, as these kids begin to recognize that they are out of step socially, they may begin to withdraw and become self-conscious, thus developing social anxiety. In such a scenario, the social anxiety develops as a result of the ADD/ADHD; however, in other cases children have both disorders that have developed independent of each other.

Whatever the situation, ADD/ADHD must be appropriately treated—and the earlier the better—so kids can catch up socially and not take such a hit to their self-esteem.

Learning disabilities. Similar to the process we described with ADD/ADHD, children with learning disabilities have difficulty taking in, storing, and retrieving information, and this can certainly affect one's social skills. Children with a learning disability have difficulty sorting through social information and as a result may make more social mistakes. They are likely to receive less than positive feedback from others, which leads to increased anxiety. This anxiety then makes them want to withdraw socially, and a vicious cycle has begun.

If you suspect that your child has learning disabilities, seek help from a qualified professional. Your child's teacher (or school counselor) may be the best person to talk with initially. Keep in mind that having a learning disability has nothing to do with intelligence. In fact, many children with a learning disability are exceedingly bright; however, they often must work harder than other kids to compensate for their different learning style.

TIPS FOR COPING WITH COEXISTING DISORDERS

IF YOU'VE RECOGNIZED your child in any of the descriptions in this chapter, you may be thinking to yourself, "How can I possibly help my child not only with social anxiety disorder but with this other problem as well?" We don't want to kid you; if your child has more than one disorder, you both face additional challenges. Here are some tips on how to deal with your situation.

Don't go it alone. This is probably the most important piece of advice we can give you. You need all the support you can get to help your child through this and maintain your sense of well-being at the same time.

Realize that self-help may not be enough. If your child is dealing with social anxiety disorder in addition to another problem, self-help approaches may not be enough. Seek a consultation with a mental health professional now, rather than spinning your wheels trying to go it alone. This doesn't mean that following the suggestions in this book isn't important. But when you're dealing with a combination of problems, approaching the situation from more than one angle is likely your best bet to ensure your child's full recovery.

Recognize the importance of the therapeutic relationship. As you know, people with social anxiety disorder desire relationships with other people but are fearful of possible rejection or disapproval. This applies to a relationship with a therapist. Before your child can make progress in treatment, he needs to feel sure that the therapist will not judge or reject him. The development of this type of trusting relationship can be a slow process for anyone but especially for kids with intense social fears.

Accept that progress may seem slow. There's no doubt it can be a struggle when your child has social anxiety disorder and another problem stacked on top. It can sometimes seem like your child isn't getting anywhere in treatment.

As a parent, you may need to examine your beliefs about the process of change, as your beliefs will likely affect your child. Do you think that therapy must proceed quickly in order to be considered successful? If you do, you're likely setting yourself—and your child—up to feel frustrated.

Although it would be nice if your child could overcome her problems quickly, it often doesn't happen so easily. If it feels as if your child is taking two steps forward and one back, that is normal. The goal is progress—even slow progress—not perfection.

Don't be afraid to try medication. There is considerable scientific evidence showing a strong biological component to anxiety disorders. For some children, even the best cognitive-behavioral therapy isn't enough. Particularly if your child is struggling with depression and anxiety, you'll want to consider medication. See Appendix A for more information on making the medication decision.

Go back to the basics. Review the general principles we presented in Chapter 3 about acceptance, patience, and focusing on the positive. Following these suggestions goes a long way toward framing things realistically and generating a healthy dose of optimism. Your child is much more than his or her anxiety disorder. With all the advances in treatment, there's every reason to believe that your child will prevail over anxiety, as well as any coexisting problems.

Make time for yourself. It can be draining and time-consuming dealing with a child who has special needs. There's a lot of running to doctor and therapy appointments, dealing with "meltdowns," helping with exposures, not to mention the other day-to-day tasks of running a family. Take a break and have some fun. Your renewed positive mental outlook will benefit not only you but also your child.

Seeking Professional Help

We hope you've made significant progress by reading this book and by teaching your child the anxiety-reduction methods we presented. However, if you need some additional guidance, the information in this appendix will show you where to begin.

WHEN SELF-HELP ISN'T ENOUGH

THERE ARE MANY times when self-help isn't enough. This is no one's fault—it's simply the case that anxiety problems tend to be complex and often coexist with other disorders, such as depression. If you have tried the strategies we outlined but haven't seen the results you hoped for, it's a good time to seek outside help.

A good first step is to visit with your family doctor or pediatrician. Anxiety can mimic several medical problems, and you want to make sure this isn't the case. Once medical problems have been ruled out, you need to find a mental health professional who works with children and who has experience treating anxiety disorders.

WHERE TO FIND HELP

THERE ARE MANY ways you can go about finding a mental health professional to work with you and your child. Read through the following list and then begin making some inquiries.

- As we mentioned, ask your family doctor or pediatrician for a referral.
- Call your insurance company or employee assistance program and ask for the names of providers.
- If there's a university medical center in your community, it may have an anxiety disorders treatment center. At the very least, it will have referral information to get you pointed in the right direction.
- Another alternative is to contact the Anxiety Disorders Association of America, which maintains a list of professionals who specialize in treating anxiety disorders. Freedom from Fear and the Association for the Advancement of Behavior Therapy are other organizations you may want to contact for referrals (see Resources).
- If you have friends or relatives who have been treated for anxiety, ask whom they saw and if they were satisfied with their treatment. Word of mouth is often an excellent means of discovering resources.
- You can always look in the yellow pages under "Psychologists" and see if there is an anxiety treatment center listed. Of course, you need to verify the individual's credentials, as anyone can advertise that he or she specializes in treating anxiety.

DIFFERENT KINDS OF DOCTORS

MANY PEOPLE ARE confused when they have to choose between a psychologist and a psychiatrist, since both usually have the title "doctor." The easiest way to distinguish between them is that psychiatrists are physicians and therefore are able to prescribe medication. Psychologists are doctors of philosophy (or of psychology) and are trained primarily in how to deliver such psychological services as psychotherapy.

Other therapists—such as social workers, psychiatric nurses, and counselors—usually have a master's degree in their area of specialization. All of these professionals may know how to conduct psychotherapy. However, it is important for you to know the specifics regarding the education and training of the professionals you are considering and whether they are licensed to practice.

How do you know if someone has the skills required to treat your child's social anxiety? The easiest way is to ask. Some people worry that they will offend professionals by asking questions about their background and training. In our experience, though, most mental health professionals are not put off by being asked to discuss their credentials. They often expect it.

QUESTIONS TO ASK

NOT EVERY MENTAL health professional has the background and training needed to work with children and adolescents suffering from social anxiety disorder. Here are some questions to ask a prospective therapist:

- Do you work with children who have anxiety disorders?
- What type of therapy do you do?
- Do you involve the parents?
- When appropriate, do you coordinate care with the primary care physician? The school?
- What type of success have you had working with these types of problems?
- How do you feel about medication? To whom do you refer patients if medication might be indicated?

- Do you recommend any particular books as an adjunct to treatment?
- Do you give assignments to complete outside the therapy sessions?
- What advanced training have you had in treating anxiety disorders in children?

Most therapists are busy, so keep your questions as focused as possible. Nonetheless, as a consumer you have the right to ask for information that will allow you to feel good about your child's care.

THE FIRST APPOINTMENT

BE SURE TO prepare your child before an initial visit with a mental health professional. Tell your child you're going to see someone who talks to children and their families and helps them with their problems. Let him know that this type of doctor doesn't give shots. For adolescents who may be embarrassed, assure them that even athletes and actors get help from psychologists, and it doesn't mean they're crazy. Also, this isn't punishment. They aren't going to a doctor because they've been "bad."

Take any questionnaires you've filled out from this book to an initial session. In particular, "Does My Child Have Social Anxiety Disorder?" from Chapter 1 will be quite helpful. The therapist may talk with you first to gain background information. Your child may or may not be present during this part of the session. If your child is with you and there is information which you need to share with the therapist privately, be sure to let the therapist know you'd like a few minutes alone with him or her.

The therapist will also, at some point, talk with your child. Again, the format of this can vary. Some therapists talk with your child privately while others have you in the room. Therapists skilled at dealing with shy, socially anxious kids are able to "read" the situation, and if the child appears uncomfortable with the idea of being separated from the parent(s), they respect this.

It may take the therapist several sessions to complete the initial assessment, gathering all the information needed to make a formal diagnosis and recommend a course of treatment. Be patient with this process. A thorough assessment is crucial to effective treatment.

WHAT TO EXPECT

ONCE YOUR CHILD has begun treatment, what should you expect? Of course, we're making generalizations, but here are some things to let you know that everyone is probably on the right track.

- One or ideally both parents are involved with the treatment process. It's typically not the case that you simply drop your child off for the therapy appointment and come back in an hour. You spend much more time with your child than the therapist does, so you need to know how to coach your child at home.
- You should feel comfortable asking the therapist questions, and you should feel that the therapist is open to this.
- Your child may take a while to warm up to the therapist, but in general, you should see increasing comfort as time goes on. On the other hand, the therapist is asking your child to do things that are scary, so take this into account when evaluating the situation. Ideally, the therapist's style is warm and encouraging, while at the same time directive.
- You and your child will probably have "homework assignments" to complete between sessions.
- It is difficult, if not impossible, to say at the outset how long treatment will last. However, every few months or so, everyone involved should discuss the progress being made and make adjustments to the treatment plan where necessary.

WHAT IF MEDICATION IS RECOMMENDED?

AT SOME POINT you may be faced with the difficult decision of whether or not to have your child try medication as a part of his or her treatment. Opinions tend to run strong on both sides of the medication issue. Many parents are naturally hesitant, if not flat-out opposed, to consider medication for their child. Usually this is due to a lack of information, as well as fear based on stories they've heard from other people or the media. Taking either extreme position—being unwilling to consider medication, or seeing it as the sole answer—will interfere with your ability to consider all the options available to your child and leave you both short-changed.

We have found that many children with social anxiety disorder can make good progress without medication, particularly if the problem is caught early and there are not a lot of complicating factors. There are times, however, when we suggest that parents seek a consultation from a child psychiatrist (or, if not available, a knowledgeable pediatrician) for their child. Some of these situations include:

- Your child is exhibiting significant depression (particularly if there are suicidal thoughts) that does not appear to be getting better with cognitive-behavioral treatment alone.
- Your child's functioning is severely affected (not attending school, for example) and the luxury of time—waiting to see if the therapy will work—is not available.
- There is no therapist available who can provide cognitive-behavioral therapy. Unfortunately, this is often the case in many rural areas.
- Your child has not made progress using cognitive-behavioral therapy alone, and a combination approach is needed.
- Your child has made some progress in therapy but needs the extra "boost" that medication can provide.

If you decide to try the medication route, your child should be monitored regularly by a physician, and the medication should be only one part of a comprehensive treatment program.

The type of medication most likely to be prescribed for your child will fall under the class of the selective serotonin reuptake inhibitors (SSRIs). Common brand names are Prozac, Zoloft, Paxil, Celexa, Luvox, and Lexapro. These medications work by increasing the availability of serotonin (a neurotransmitter that affects mood and anxiety) in the brain. When an SSRI is properly prescribed and monitored, medication can be very helpful. Your doctor can explain the potential benefits (and possible side effects) of any medication.

In considering the possibility of medication for your child, we encourage you to ask your physician the following questions:

- How does this medication work?
- What are the potential benefits for my child?
- What type of side effects might I see?
- When should my child take the medicine?
- How and how soon will I know it's working?
- How long will my child need to take the medication?

SSRIs may take several weeks to work, and their initial impact may be rather subtle. We frequently encourage parents and the child to assess the medication's effectiveness by having the child rate his mood and anxiety levels daily after starting medication. You can keep this information on a calendar or journal and bring this data to the doctor for follow-up appointments. This allows you some objectivity in measuring the improvement over time and helps you recognize even small increments of progress.

While SSRIs are the most commonly used medications for social anxiety, your doctor may want to consider other classes of medication for specific circumstances. Your doctor should be able to provide you with the rationale behind choosing a specific medication.

If medication is suggested for your child, keep an open mind and do some research. A good book on the subject is *Straight Talk About Psychiatric Medications for Kids* (see Resources).

Resources

Below are lists of books, organizations, and Web sites that you may find useful in your efforts to help your child overcome shyness and social anxiety. Knowledge truly is a source of power—make good use of the resources available to you.

BOOKS

Anxiety Disorders

Rapee, Ronald M., Susan H. Spence, Vanessa Cobham, and Ann Wignall. *Helping Your Anxious Child: A Step-by-Step Guide for Parents.* Oakland, CA: New Harbinger Publications, 2000. Solid information on the cognitive-behavioral treatment of childhood anxiety disorders.

Ross, Jerilyn. *Triumph Over Fear: A Book of Help and Hope for People with Anxiety, Panic Attacks, and Phobias.* New York: Bantam Books, 1994.

An inspiring and practical book written by the president of the *Anxiety Disorders Association of America*. Contains a chapter on diagnosing and treating children.

Wagner, Aureen Pinto. *Worried No More: Help and Hope for Anxious Children*. Rochester, NY: Lighthouse Press, 2002.
Very comprehensive. Contains useful information for teachers, as well as parents.

Children and Parenting

Kurcinka, Mary Sheedy. *Raising Your Spirited Child*. New York: HarperCollins, 1991.
A lifesaving guide on understanding and working with your child's temperament. Highly recommended.

Turecki, Stanley. *The Emotional Problems of Normal Children: How Parents Can Understand and Help*. New York: Bantam Books, 1994.
A reassuring book on how every child can have problems and how parents can help. Good information on the topics of communication and effective discipline. Also offers tips on knowing when to seek professional help.

Depression

Koplewicz, Harold S. *More than Moody: Recognizing and Treating Adolescent Depression*. New York: Putnam, 2002.

Miller, Jeffrey A. *The Childhood Depression Sourcebook*. Lincolnwood, IL: Lowell House, 1999.

Medication

Gorman, Jack M. *The Essential Guide to Psychiatric Drugs*. New York: St. Martin's Press, 1998.

A good reference for commonly prescribed psychiatric drugs. Updated frequently.

Wilens, Timothy E. *Straight Talk About Psychiatric Medications for Kids.* New York: Guilford Press, 1999.

Obsessive-Compulsive Disorder

Wagner, Aureen Pinto. *Up and Down the Worry Hill: A Children's Book About Obsessive-Compulsive Disorder and Its Treatment.* Rochester, NY: Lighthouse Press, 2000.

Wagner, Aureen Pinto. *What to Do When Your Child Has Obsessive-Compulsive Disorder: Strategies and Solutions.* Rochester, NY: Lighthouse Press, 2002.

Waltz, Mitzi. *Obsessive-Compulsive Disorder: Help for Children and Adolescents.* N. Sebastopol, CA: O'Reilly & Associates, 2000.

Selective Mutism

Visit www.selectivemutism.org.

Sensory Integration Dysfunction

Kranowitz, Carol Stock. *The Out-of-Sync Child: Recognizing and Coping with Sensory Integration Dysfunction.* New York: Berkley, 1998.

Shyness/Social Anxiety/Social Phobia

Berent, Jonathan. *Beyond Shyness: How to Conquer Social Anxieties.* New York: Simon & Schuster, 1993.
Particularly useful information for parents seeking help for adolescents and grown children with social anxiety disorder. Guides parents in empowering their children to accept responsibility and differentiates between nurturing and rescuing.

Carducci, Bernardo J. *Shyness: A Bold New Approach.* New York: HarperCollins, 1999.
Contains information on shyness throughout the life cycle. Carducci reassures parents that shy children aren't destined to be shy adults.

Carducci, Bernardo J. *The Shyness Breakthrough: A No-Stress Plan to Help Your Shy Child Warm Up, Open Up, and Join the Fun.* Emmaus, PA: Rodale, 2003.
Another excellent book by Carducci. Shows you how to help your child lead a "successfully shy" life.

Markway, Barbara G., Cheryl N. Carmin, C. Alec Pollard, and Teresa Flynn. *Dying of Embarrassment: Help for Social Anxiety & Phobia.* Oakland, CA: New Harbinger Publications, 1992.
The first self-help book written on social anxiety/phobia, it's still must reading for anyone serious about understanding this condition.

Markway, Barbara G., and Gregory P. Markway. *Painfully Shy: How to Overcome Social Anxiety and Reclaim Your Life.* New York: St. Martin's Press, 2001.
Written primarily for adults with social anxiety disorder. Adolescents will also benefit from reading it.

Schneier, Franklin, and Lawrence Welkwitz. *The Hidden Face of Shyness: Understanding and Overcoming Social Anxiety.* New York: Avon Books, 1996.
Effectively combines research findings with case histories to provide an excellent account of the nature and treatment of social anxiety. Chapter 17 includes information on parenting the shy child.

Stein, Murray B., and John R. Walker. *Triumph over Shyness*. New York: McGraw-Hill, 2002.
Includes a short chapter on parenting the shy child.

Swallow, Ward K. *The Shy Child: Helping Children Triumph over Shyness*. New York: Warner Books, 2000.
Good information on how shyness presents itself at each developmental stage of the child's life.

For children's books on shyness, see www.parentingpress.com, www.polaris.nova.edu/~malouffj/shyness.htm, and shykids.com.

ORGANIZATIONS

American Academy of Child and Adolescent Psychiatry
3615 Wisconsin Avenue, NW
Washington, DC 20016
800-333-7636
www.aacap.org

American Psychiatric Association
1400 K Street, NW
Washington, DC 20005
(202) 682-6220
www.psych.org

American Psychological Association
750 First Street, NE
Washington, DC 20002-4242
(202) 336-5500
www.apa.org

Anxiety Disorders Association of America
6000 Executive Blvd., Dept. A
Rockville, MD 20852-2624
(301) 231-9350
www.adaa.org

Association for the Advancement of Behavior Therapy (AABT)
305 Seventh Avenue, 16th floor
New York, NY 10001-6008
212-647-1890
www.aabt.org

National Alliance for the Mentally Ill
200 N. Glebe Road, Suite 1015
Arlington, VA 22203-3754
(800) 950-NAMI
www.nami.org

Obsessive-Compulsive Foundation
PO Box 9573
New Haven, CT 06535
(203)315-2190
www.ocfoundation.org

WEB SITES

The Internet can be a valuable source of information on social anxiety disorder. Keep in mind, though, that it is not a substitute for advice from your physician or a mental health professional.

We reviewed these sites and found them to be user-friendly and full of helpful information. However, because of the rapidly changing Internet environment, it's possible that some of these sites will be inactive by the time you are reading this.

Also, particularly in chat rooms or on e-mail lists, misinformaiton abounds. Realize that not everything you read will be factually correct.

American Academy of Child and Adolescent of Psychiatry
www.aacap.org

American Psychiatric Association
www.psych.org

American Psychological Association
www.apa.org

Anxiety Disorders Association of America
www.adaa.org

Anxiety Network International
www.anxietynetwork.com

Association for the Advancement of Behavior Therapy
www.aabt.org

Canadian Psychiatric Association
http://cpa.medical.org

Cognitive Therapy
www.cognitivetherapy.com

Freedom from Fear
www.freedomfromfear.org

Internet Mental Health
www.mentalhealth.com

Markway, Greg and Barbara
www.markway.com

Mayo Clinic
www.mayohealth.org

National Depressive and Manic-Depressive Web Site
http://www.ndmda.org

Open Mind
www.open-mind.org/SP/

Painfully Shy
www.painfullyshy.com

Panic/Anxiety Disorders
www.panicdisorder.about.com

Selective Mutism Group
www.selectivemutism.org

Shy and Free
http://www.shyandfree.com

Shy Kids
www.shykids.com

Social Anxiety Network
www.social-anxiety-network.com

Social Anxiety Organization
www.social-anxiety.org